OK, You're a New Executive.

Now What?

OK, You're a New Executive. Now What?

Reflections on 40 years of executive experiences in small corporations

By

Jack Marino PE

This book is dedicated to my children and their families. John, Kathy and her husband Bill, Sheila, Tricia and her husband George, Tom and his wife Patty, and Mattie and her husband Lance and our sixteen grandchildren that they may find something in this text that can help them in their careers.

Copyright © 2017 by John A. Marino

ISBN-13 978-15427229673

Printed in the United States of America

Acknowledgments

My career could not have happened without the support of my wife, Jean. She managed the home front and our six children amidst many moves to new localities and my intense travel schedules.

None of this would have happened without the great engineering education I received from my alma mater, Rensselaer Polytechnic Institute.

Early in my career, I was fortunate to work for John Gerdes, the owner of Hauck Manufacturing, when I joined his company in 1967. He had vision and faith in the new technology I brought for the design of the Hauck "Turboblower."

When I embarked on the contract to purchase Denton, the advice and council of Seymour Shiroki, a brilliant accountant and partner, was invaluable toward my understanding of finance.

Louis Etschemaier was president of Hauck in 1998 when he offered me a position as a Senior Vice President as part of his goal in restoring Hauck. We had a great run together.

I also had so many talented engineers, salesmen, technicians, and factory mechanics who worked for me that made my job such a joy.

Many thanks to my friends at *Industrial Heating* magazine, who encouraged me when I retired to write blogs for their website, which has led to this book.

Finally, I have a debt of gratitude to Beth Levan, a longtime friend, who, as my editor, gathered what started out as random blogs and put them together to form this book.

Contents

Preface..1

Introduction...5

Chapter 1. The New Executive at Work……........9

Chapter 2. Making a Business Plan……………...31

Chapter 3. Understanding Financial Statements…53

Chapter 4. Managing Marketing and Sales……….71

Chapter 5. Developing New Products……………81

Chapter 6. Dealing with Dishonesty……………..93

Chapter 7. Leadership in Times of Crisis………...107

Chapter 8. When Owners and Managers Fail…..119

Chapter 9. The Impact of the New Technologies………………………………….127

Chapter 10. What Might the Future Bring?.........135

Appendix…………………………………….151

Bibliography…………………………………167

About the Author……………………………163

Preface

This book is written for those who are promoted into a senior management role from one of the operating departments in a smaller company. It also is intended to help those who are joining the management team in a small company after having worked in a mega corporation. If this is you, you may or may not have had any real management training, but certainly, you will confront day-to-day problems that are different from those you had been used to solving. During my career, I have participated in everything from product development to personnel problems and from corporate and department budgets to board of director's meetings. It is my hope that some of the insights I obtained in going from a technical engineering life to the full responsibility of corporate management in smaller companies will help you do your job more efficiently.

My professional career began after graduating with a bachelor's degree in engineering. Following a stint as an Army artillery officer, I started work at Pratt & Whitney in East Hartford, Connecticut. I spent five years there working on jet engines. But I found the aerospace industry to be too big and confining, so I went to work for a small privately-held manufacturing company. From there, I was recruited by another small manufacturing company in Pennsylvania to design a new line of turbo machinery, and that's where my management experience began.

My work resulted in several U.S. patents and a product line that provided the biggest margin in the company's line of products. That product is still selling some 45 years after its introduction. That success led to my promotion to chief engineer and then to vice president, engineering when I was 39 years old. A couple of years later, I also took on the role of vice president of sales. During that time, I took evening classes and received a master's degree in engineering. After ten years, I left that company following a management dispute over the company's future.

From there, I did some consulting work before beginning discussions with the owner of a privately-owned company in Syracuse, New York, who wished to sell and retire. The company was engaged in technology like that of the company I had left in Pennsylvania. I negotiated a deal to buy out his interest and, with another investor's backing, took over as president and CEO. The company had been poorly managed and was struggling. During this time, I also took the New York tests and passed for certification as a professional engineer, which I figured would help our company in some of its projects. We slimmed down, reorganized our sales personnel, improved our manufacturing capabilities, and started to make real headway.

Unfortunately, no sooner did we get things under control than the recession of the early 1990's struck hard on the manufacturing industries. The local bank that held our line of credit and a loan also was sold to a big regional bank. Shortly thereafter, I got a call from the VP of the bank saying that it was going to call in all of our notes in 30 days!

We kept them at bay for almost six months, holding on to our customers and personnel with minimum operating money. Meanwhile, I put together a deal to sell the company to a large privately-held environmental consulting engineering company that was looking to broaden its business model beyond environmental consulting. The bank got its money, and I agreed to stay on as manager of the business.

A few years later, my former employer in Pennsylvania came calling. That business had been sold to a German company and had undergone several management changes. The new president had no experience in that industry and was looking for technical industry experience. We reached an agreement, and in 1998, at 60 years old, I returned. The next 10 years were some of the most productive years of my career. We developed whole lines of new products, overhauled our operating systems by installing new SAP software, and led the opening of our very successful sales effort in mainland China. I retired as senior VP at age 70.

It is from these experiences that I've drawn upon to share my thoughts on what it takes to be a manager in a smaller independently-owned business. Managing in this environment is vastly different than in a large mega corporation with its many resources. It can also be a lot more fun and rewarding – not necessarily monetarily – but definitely in the full sense of accomplishment.

Readers of this book will find no new management principles revealed or any of the latest buzz words. However, it is my hope that somewhere in this book, I can give you some insight that will help you manage and be more successful, as well as keep your company a part of the great American landscape.

Introduction

For the purposes of this book, I chose to define the small company as having up to 500 employees. My experience has been in manufacturing in companies of this size, but a great deal of what I will discuss in this book can apply to many other types of work. As a senior manager in this environment, you may have two or three other managers at your level, and all of you will be responsible for all aspects of running that business. In a similar position in a very large corporation, most of the tasks you would have to manage would be taken care of by a large staff of specialists, and your actual knowledge of these activities would be very limited. Your freedom to innovate would also be quite different.

The small business may be led by the principal owner, who acts as CEO, or it may have a president hired by non-active owners. In that case, you may even be that president. These companies may make a profit of 10% to 15% on sales, which will usually flow back to the owners/stockholders after possible distribution of profit sharing. Unlike the mega corporations, manager salaries are relatively proportional to the average employee. These are your traditional American small businesses. Managers *and* employees likely live in the same communities, and their children most likely will attend the same schools and play on teams together. Several generations of a family also may have worked for or are currently employees of the company. Fortunately, some of those places still exist, but they have certainly been threatened.

All companies, but particularly those in this category, are dependent on the concept of four essential elements of a successful business. The elements are a product, customers, finance, and employees. The product could be either a physical item or a service but something that has value to potential customers either way. Of course, without customers who will buy your product, there is no business. Capital investment and operating expenses are dependent on the financial health of the enterprise. But a good manager should not overlook the importance of loyal and knowledgeable employees. In many cases, for these small operations, much of the real product and operational knowhow resides in these people. These are the traditional middle-class workers, who have been dealt such a bad hand with the trend toward globalization and outsourcing as smaller companies are gobbled up by mega corporations. Many employees become mere pawns that can be replaced by other pawns somewhere in the new organization. Or their jobs are eliminated because that department is relocated to some other remote location within the tentacles of the corporation – maybe even in another country. Or whole categories of what are determined to be "non-essential" activities are outsourced to companies specializing in that activity.

What happens to innovation when creative people get mired in the new bureaucracy? That is exactly why innovations in America come almost always from small companies. Historically, very few ideas that change an industry are hatched by the mega giant whose ultimate goal usually is to protect the vested interests of the financial community. The examples are everywhere.

In the autonomous small company, if you are the top sales executive, as part of the corporate team, you will likely get involved with many sticky personnel problems or plans to rework the manufacturing or assembly operation. With all the employee rules and regulations, hopefully you do have a key knowledgeable person assigned to personnel problems. If you're the top guy in engineering, you must have intimate knowledge of how your products are manufactured, sold, and used. Each of you and your senior cohorts will be responsible for corporate budgets as well as department budgets. This group will also be responsible for plotting the long-range goals, new product needs, new market possibilities and marketing strategies. There likely will be no economist or attorney on your staff.

When the economy enters a recession – which it surely will and probably more than once in your career as a manager – you need to know what steps to take and what things to avoid to survive the downturn. Your knowledge of financial statements will be tested, perhaps as part of your participation in board of directors' meetings.

So, if you are a key manager in one of these small entrepreneurial companies, take heart. You won't probably be paid as well as those in mega land, but you will have much satisfaction in seeing the results of your input – that is until your company is sold out to either the financial community or a mega corporation. If you stay on after the sale, your life will definitely change.

Chapter 1.
The New Executive at Work

"The Effective Executive." That is the title of a classic book by one of my favorite management consultants – Peter Drucker. He wrote this book in 1966, but its principles are as valid today as ever, maybe even more so. I'll discuss this volume and other works by this now deceased genius periodically.

Drucker identifies five habits that must be acquired to be an effective executive. And in times of turmoil, as an executive, you will need to have these habits or else develop them quickly.

1. Know where your time goes. In many cases, your time will be eaten up by the demands of others. Therefore, getting control of the time you have left is imperative.
2. Focus on getting results rather than work. Focus on what is expected of you and the goals that are set for the company.
3. Build on your strengths and the strengths of your subordinates. Do not try to build on weaknesses. Focus on what your organization can do effectively. Make use of the people in your organization who have the required expertise, and be sure they have enough authority to get results.
4. Concentrate on those areas where superior performance can bring outstanding results.

Do the first things first and the second things not at all. Don't let the flow of events determine what you take seriously. Don't manage from your "in box" less you fritter away your time "operating." I personally have observed that this is the biggest mistake a new manager will make.
5. Make few but very fundamental decisions. Making too many decisions fast also means making too many very wrong decisions. An effective decision is almost always a judgment based on dissenting opinions not consensus. Some decisions will still be wrong, and you must be ready to adopt an alternative direction quickly. I've always held that your original decisions should be right at least 80% of the time.

The important events that you must focus on are not the trends but those changes in the paradigms that are coming today. You need to look outside of the company to understand what is needed. Focusing too much on the inside will blind you to the changing realities.

I spent a great deal of my career in a small manufacturing company managing an engineering department. I grew up as an engineer in combustion and heat transfer. I remember a job interview I took early in my career with a high-tech builder of rocket engines. I think I was being interviewed by the chief engineer. He gave me a very simple problem to solve. An engine bracket was experiencing fatigue cracking along a flange. How would you analyze the problem? What would be the recommended fix?

My answer eliminated me from the list of candidates. The best answer I could come up with was "make it thicker." No analysis, just beef it up. Of course, I knew I had blown it immediately. But it made me realize how important my technical training had been and how much of it I had probably ignored in my day-to-day work. I vowed never again to avoid the proper technical analysis, but I also made a note that when I became a manager, I would demand technical competence from my staff.

What I have observed in engineers is that many of us grew up with lots of hands-on mechanics. We like to think we can fix anything. In many cases, that is why we studied engineering in college. Of course, once in college, we discovered that to be an engineer, you had to be a complete master of mathematics. Many couldn't deal with that and changed majors. Others managed to just get through but went back to being mechanics when they graduated, glad to escape all that math. Going back to being a mechanic is a career-ending mistake.

If you are an engineering manager, you must demonstrate first that you are a master of the technology your company manufactures. Then, you must insist that your staff rise to that same level. They must be able to apply the basic fundamentals of their training to the everyday problems for which their expertise is required.

So, have you figured out a better answer to the engine bracket problem? I'll give you a more thorough analysis than "make it thicker," even though that still might be the final answer. A bracket on an engine was cracking from fatigue. How would you solve the problem? First of all, you should verify that it is indeed fatigue that is causing the problem. Examining the surface of the crack will tell you that quickly. Consulting references for the particular material will usually include pictures of various types of fractures. Once you've verified the cause, that same reference will also give you the stress level at which cyclical fatigue will be experienced. Knowing the stress level, one can then back calculate the moment of inertia of the failed section that will reduce the stress to a lower level. There are, of course, other approaches as well, such as reducing the level of the applied stress. The key is to start with an analysis that brings you to a logical solution. The old "hack and whack" approach to problem solving is far too expensive in today's world. You do not want those kinds of engineers on your staff.

Since I spent my career in heat processing, I'll use this technology to illustrate some points. In the industrial heating business, heat implies the concept of enthalpy. Remember that from your old thermodynamics courses? Well, you might be surprised at how many engineers in this business can't explain that concept. I've used that question many times during interviews with job applicants. Even some new graduates have forgotten what it means.

The very words "industrial heating" imply the fundamental concept of heat transfer. Obviously, to heat one substance means transferring heat to that substance from another source. You can't get very far in understanding heat transfer if you've forgotten about enthalpy. Heat transfer itself can involve many difficult calculations. The formulae can be very complicated, and since it implies by its very nature a transient state, differential calculus is involved if you need an exact solution. But rarely do we need an exact solution to that degree in our day-to-day problem solving. So how do we get answers?

Computer programs today handle much of this analysis. But how can you apply these programs to constantly changing everyday problems? Basically, you can't. Many years ago, when I attended a meeting of the American Flame Research Committee (AFRC), I met Professor Hoyt Hottel, then retired from MIT. Professor Hottel, besides being one of the founders of the AFRC, was one of the great minds that developed a great deal of the modern radiant heat transfer analysis along with much of the basic research in radiant heat transfer from gases. Only at the end of his career did the earliest computers become available for scientific research. So, his work was done the hard way.

The lasting comment that Professor Hottel left me with during his discussion was that you had to be able to handle the most complicated analysis with simple concepts that you could calculate "on the back of an envelope." Otherwise, how could you have any faith in a computer printout? As we all know – garbage in, garbage out. So as a manager of complex technology, how do you know if the results you or your staff gets make any sense? Without an understanding of the very basic fundamentals, you don't.

Let's take an example of how a "back of the envelope" calculation might give you insight into one of the most controversial discussions of our time – global warming. Many very smart scientists have developed what must be very complex computer programs that calculate the effect of CO_2 emissions from man-made sources on the temperature of our atmosphere. Seems like something this complex would not lend itself to a simple analysis. But is that true?

To begin with, let's look at the composition of our atmosphere, which is heated by the sun and, by radiant heat transfer, transfers additional heat to the earth's surface. Now radiant heat transfer is something an engineer in the heat processing industry understands well. For instance, we all know that in a furnace atmosphere, any nitrogen or oxygen in the atmosphere has no impact on the radiant heat transfer since both have zero emissivity. The primary radiant energy is generated by the CO_2 and water vapor in the combustion gases.

From the 1976 Standard Atmosphere Tables generated by the government, we know that 99% of the atmosphere is made up of oxygen and nitrogen. The trace elements present are the only elements that contribute to any radiant heat transfer from the atmosphere to the surface. From those tables, CO_2

has a presence of 322 ppm. Up to an altitude of 2 km, water vapor (w.v.) is present at an average concentration of 2843 ppm. Now, from our knowledge of the science of radiation and using standard emissivity tables, we also know that water vapor has about 2.3 times the emissivity of CO_2.

From these global warming discussions, we are told that about 3-4% of the CO_2 in the atmosphere comes from man-made sources. But let's say it may even be as high as 5%, or 16 ppm. Now let's make our "back of the envelope" calculation. With w.v. having 2.3 times the impact on radiation of CO_2, the impact of the man-made CO_2 to radiant heat transfer in our atmosphere is $(16 \times 1/2843 \times 2.3) \times 100 = 0.24\%$ of the total. And if we eliminated all the man-made CO_2, the impact on the atmospheric radiation from the combined effect of the CO_2 and w.v. would be a reduction of about 0.23%. $[16 \times 1/(2843 \times 2.3 + 322 \times 1)]$.

Of course, all the man-made CO_2 cannot be totally eliminated, so does anyone really believe that with all the variables involved in using average concentrations in the world's atmosphere and eliminating all the impact of variations in the sun itself that this would have any impact? Does this computer program calculate the impact of all the explosives from WWII and Vietnam or the 2,120 atomic bombs detonated in the atmosphere and in the Pacific Ocean? As a manager, what faith would you have in the result predicted from these programs? How much of your company's future would you put at risk from these results? Unless, of course, there was government funding involved.

When I entered my professional life, we didn't have calculators. Computers, when they did exist, were confined to the accounting department for payroll and accounting calculations. We used slide rules. Most of you reading this have no idea how they work, but leave it to say, you multiply and divide by adding and subtracting logarithms. Therefore, you had no evaluation on where the decimal point belonged. You had to carry in your head the order of magnitude of each calculation. This turned out to be great discipline for evaluating computer results.

All of my earliest designs were done on a slide rule. Very complicated heat transfer and fluid flow formulae were reduced to simpler models that could easily be handled with slide rule simplicity and accuracy. You can basically read only three significant figures on a slide rule. If you can recall, in the movie *Apollo 13,* when the engineers at the Johnson Space Center had to make rapid calculation about the new trajectory and power use following the explosion aboard the spacecraft, they were using slide rules!

Today, of course, one has a pocket calculator that is more powerful than the computers available to the designers of the Apollo program. However, making simple calculations using just basic concepts can provide you with much insight as to whether that giant computer program or CFD picture makes any sense. As an engineering manager, you need to know how to use simplified calculations. As a manager of technology, you must make sure that your staff stays current with the latest technology. Provide them with the latest tools, such as CFD modeling. Make sure they read current literature and attend appropriate seminars in their fields.

When I was a graduate student taking advanced thermodynamics and heat transfer courses, I was also working a full-time job as a project engineer. To keep current in the technology, I read numerous papers in the field. What I discovered in reading these papers was that the authors started from a point where the concept they were exploring had already been mathematically developed and went on from there to develop their thesis. When discussing this with my professor, I suggested that a real-world situation could be developed for the students (most of whom were just out of their bachelor programs) by having them select current papers and write an assignment summarizing the basic concepts that led up to the new details and present that to the class. He really liked the idea; unfortunately, I was not thought of kindly by the rest of the class! As a technology manager, how would your staff fare with this exercise?

The key to managing a successful engineering activity or department is to manage the innovation of the key members of that organization. Referring once again to Drucker in another of his books, *Innovation and Entrepreneurship*, he outlines a number of issues important to managers of technology.

1. Innovation. Identify your customer needs and develop products to meet them.

Differentiate your company's products from your competitors'. Focus on the technology. Understand it thoroughly, and apply it intelligently.
2. Personnel. Surround yourself with the best people you can hire. Develop and cultivate their loyalty. Allow them to make their mistakes. Nurture the mavericks in your group. They may be hard to manage, but give them their space – from them will likely come your best ideas.
3. Vision. Know where you are going and always lead the way. Make sure your company has a strategic plan. You will be the bridge between your development group and the rest of the company management. This will prove to be very difficult at times – particularly at times when budgets are being cut.

One of the keys to developing successful new products is to find the specialized niches in your industry. When you find that niche, move into it at full speed with all the resources you can muster. This is a great gamble of course, and it will be unforgiving if you make no allowances for a mistake. Usually, there will be no second chance.
    In the practice of providing heat for industrial processes, new technology is not readily accepted. Because the application of heat in manufacturing is so basic to the whole process, the failure of a new product or process applied in the manufacturing cycle can have catastrophic impact

on the entire plant's production. The product associated with that failure will be totally rejected. No amount of marketing effort will erase that memory for a very long time. So be sure you have carefully tested any new technology as close to actual conditions as you can. Don't overlook those small failures that occur under lab conditions as unimportant. When subject to operations under uncontrolled conditions at a 24/7 pace, that small failure will likely become a much larger factor.

Once, while discussing new technology we were applying at a Nucor Steel plant, a corporate VP told me they experimented constantly with new ideas. That vision has undoubtedly made Nucor a leader in the industry. He stated, however, that they had broken up more concrete in one year associated with failed new technology than most steel plants had installed. That's great, but you don't want your products lying in the bone yard behind the Nucor plant.

Talking About Raises and Performance Reviews

If you currently find yourself in a recession, your company probably hasn't given out too many performance raises. But as business picks up, some of your key people are already lining up their thoughts on asking for that raise. There are always periodic articles about, as an employee, how to ask the boss for a raise. These include things like asking for a personal meeting, being assertive, being informed about your market value and keeping cool during the meeting. Great. But how do you, as the boss, handle these meetings?

A corollary to these meetings might be the annual performance review meeting you, as the boss, are supposed to conduct with your people. In my opinion, the annual performance review is one of the most ill-conceived ideas given us by the management gurus. Unbelievably, many companies still conduct these useless exercises. The idea should be put out of its misery once and for all. Management hates them, and employees hate them.

Don't get me wrong, reviewing performance is a good thing, but it should be done at the appropriate time when there is a reason to discuss the actual results of a person's work. Such times, for example, are when a project has achieved its goals, there has been a successful sales initiative, or there has been a failure in these areas. That is when the performance review will be most effective and will be most believable to the employee.

I know that Jack Welch, former chairman and CEO of General Electric, credited with that company's superb growth during his administration, has said that you promote the top 20% of your people and rid your company of the bottom 20% of performers. But I don't think I've ever read exactly how he made those distinctions. I do suspect that GE used the annual performance review somewhere in its businesses. If so, I wonder how important that really was, and I seriously doubt Welch used those reviews (if they had any) for selecting his top performers.

As a manager giving out performance reviews, you know that you cannot give everyone who works for you a top grade. Even if your department has all of the company's top performers, you cannot have that show in your results. In this silly exercise, someone or several will have to finish below average. The result could be an enormous amount of damage to your company's future if these top performers given low ratings have to leave your company in order to realize their potential.

So, what do you do instead of these annual reviews? As a manager of a department or operation, you know which people make things happen and which are merely hanging on. If you don't, you need to spend less time at your desk and more time out where the action is in your department.

Have conversations, a rarity in many companies. By talking with your people, you find out what motivates them or maybe find out there's a personal problem at home that is keeping them from performing at their best. By talking to them, you can also convey the vision of the future you, as the senior manager, see for the company with the success of their project or operation. That is so critical. Particularly when a person's project is mired in a rut or beset by technical difficulties, a refreshing discussion on how that project will fit into the company's future can help re-motivate that person's efforts. Or maybe as you listen to the problems, you may have suggestions to offer from your own experiences. I have found this to work on many occasions.

During these conversations, you can also discuss with your top performers your plans for where they can go in the next couple of years if the company's success continues. This will do more for your group's morale than any annual performance review could ever achieve. Of course, the goals you lay out have got to be believable for that employee – no pie-in-the-sky dreams that they've been hearing for years without ever seeing any real results. When your slower performers are in difficulties, these conversations can show your dissatisfaction with their progress. The options you will lay out for these people will not be as attractive, of course. Hopefully, the conversation will lead to positive changes instead. Periodic conversations with your people at key times in their assignments will prove to have a far greater impact on their performance and will provide you with more information as to who is really achieving results for the company.

Armed with this information, you are much better prepared to handle the "Boss, I deserve a raise" meeting. First of all, most employees probably don't understand how raises are really handled in your company. In their mind, you, as the boss of a department or division, have a pool of money from which you can issue any raise if you so desire. Even though they probably see it and work with it on a regular basis, they don't tie in your department's operating budget with their need for a raise.

In my experiences, the only person in a company that doesn't have a budget is the CEO. He can authorize expenditures for any project or raise he sees fit to undertake with the company's final figures being his only restraint. As a department or division manager, you have no such authority. Unless you have already had raises pre-approved in your operating budget, you probably have little leeway to honor that request for more money. So, what do you do?

If your employee is following the procedures outlined by the management gurus, he or she is first going to try to understand where you are coming from. If you are a good manager, this should not be a very difficult assignment for them. You will have had enough interaction with the employee such that he will know what kind of personality he is dealing with. If you have put your stamp on the group you manage, giving a forthright answer should end the interview right there if the answer is "there are no raises in our budget at this time." If you do have money available, let him know you are open to a discussion.

If the situation with the company is not good, the employee should already know this. Reminding him of this should put the discussion to rest. The employee will probably then want to show you how he is worth more, even in this situation. Obviously, even if you are sympathetic to the request, the probability is that you have no money available. That should once again end the discussion about money, but you should hear out the employee's position so that you totally understand what is motivating the request.

In many companies, raises and promotions are handed out at the same time throughout the company. You may have given this employee the generally agreed to cost-of-living increase; however, he may believe he is being underpaid and wants to present a case for more money.

One of the worst offenses your employee can make is to come in armed with what he considers to be the equivalent income at a similar company or with information about what another employee in another department is being paid. Certainly, the implication is that he's been looking around or has another offer.

That should definitely be a show stopper, and you should begin to plan on his or her replacement right then and there. You might also want to find out how he obtained information about another employee. If it is not true and based on hearsay, you should correct the record right away. But the only appropriate answer is "not at this time." If you give in and permit a raise as a stop gap measure, what are you going to say to the person when you do find a replacement and have the termination discussion? You have put yourself in the position of having given a raise to someone you plan to terminate, opening the company to a possible wrongful-termination case.

In other cases, they are using standard industry publications or surveys. While these can be useful, they cannot be used easily to compare your company against some sort of broad industry survey. It's the classic apples-and-oranges comparison.

There are times when the employee knows he can't make any more money in his present job and will ask for more responsibility. Here, you have to carefully examine that person's qualifications for the promotion and outline the steps that he will have to take to get there or perhaps look for the right opportunity to place him in that higher position.

Of course, the much easier task is that you do agree with the need for more money and the company has the budget to support that need. That's the easy part of management.

How's Your Company's Morale?

One day, you are going to find your company in the grip of either a general economic recession or a significant decline in customer sales for one reason or another. As a manager, you are now faced with a serious challenge that may even impact your company's survival. You have probably had all the layoffs and early retirements that you can tolerate. Are you using the company-wide furlough? That one week every other month or so, including the highest executives, will save a lot of cash and keep your core together. All this is going to have an impact on the company morale. This will be particularly true if the hourly workers have been bearing the brunt of the terminations. However, there are some things that you can do to help the situation.

Make sure that everyone is impacted. If the troops know that the top people in the company are also having pay reductions, either by furloughs or other means, they will appreciate that the burden is being shared. Don't forget, everyone is in this boat together.

Share the company's operating data. Have small department meetings, and share the company's operating statement for the last month or quarter. Show how expense cuts have impacted the bottom line. Share the latest sales figures. Talk about the latest projects won or the latest developments in R&D for that new product that will be ready when the economy recovers. There's always some good news even in the darkest times.

Recognize good work. Even without the extra cash for bonuses, employees will appreciate being recognized for extra work efforts. Identify those who have gone beyond the norm in meetings or with pictures and bulletins.

Use some time for more education. Outside education budgets have probably been cut, but there are ways to provide continuing education without much cost. Use your in-house expertise to provide education in relevant subjects for some of the junior staff and hourly employees. Upgrading their knowledge about your technology will pay off when times are good and be a morale booster in this economy.

Staying Motivated

I had the opportunity to hear Rudolph Giuliani discuss his visions on leadership. Giuliani is the former mayor of New York, and after the 9/11 attacks, he became known as "America's Mayor" as a result of his performance during that crisis. I'd like to share some of his vision with you. The following is from notes I took during one of his presentations.

Giuliani believes that to be a strong leader, you must have strong beliefs and goals. In his discussion, he reminded the audience that President Ronald Reagan had two unflinching beliefs that he applied to his role as president – communism is evil and his faith in God. Giuliani decided early in his life to apply his own faith to real-world situations, which meant fighting for what was right and moral. As a prosecutor, he went after the Mafia and corruption even though it was very dangerous to do so.

Be an optimist and a problem solver. After 9/11, Giuliani had some doubts about how the spirit of the city would survive the disaster. But he shoved those doubts out of his mind and took an optimistic approach. Pessimistic leaders, he knew, always fail. "Fear paralyzes. Hope mobilizes."

Courage will overcome fear, and unexpected things will happen. Obstacles appear in your path every day. At each obstacle, you are forced to choose. How will you react? Each time you dig in and get the job done, you make progress and prepare yourself for the next test. Determination inspires others.

Be prepared for the unexpected. During the attack, he was trapped when the first tower collapsed. He tried to escape through the basement, but the doors were locked. He told himself, "Keep your composure. Focus on the next choice. Make it a wise one." As the saying goes, "Don't sweat the small stuff." If you worry about the small day-to-day events, you won't be prepared for the big ones.

Learn from others wiser than yourself. Giuliani claims he changed more from his bout with prostate cancer than from 9/11. Having to deal with cancer gave him more wisdom about the value of life and how little control we have over death. He believes we can spare ourselves some pain by learning from the wisdom of others. We learn from our parents, our friends and everyone we meet. We learn from those we don't meet through study, prayer and reflection. He reads biographies of people he admires to see how they faced adversity. Wisdom can be gained from every conversation. "Courageous people are lifelong learners and apply wisdom from the difficult situations they encounter."

Have compassion and love – look beyond yourself. Giuliani came to believe from his time as mayor that it is better to be respected than to be loved. However, the 9/11 attacks unlocked a compassion within him that he had previously only shared with this family. He discovered that reveling your love and compassion doesn't weaken your leadership. It makes it stronger. Love helps one to look beyond what's best for ourselves and focus on what's best for others. "Love – not duty – is what makes a firefighter run into a flaming building to save someone he or she has never met."

Mayor Giuliani's thoughts are very important to one's development as a true leader. There is no magic formula, of course. However, the choices you make in life, as our parents always told us, will have an impact on your life. Make those choices count and develop your character.

Chapter 2.
Making a Business Plan

The U.S. economy, as we all know, is quite cyclical. We get four or five years of great economic activity followed by a downturn that can dramatically impact a company's bottom line. Anticipating these cyclical changes is one of the more important functions you, as a corporate manager, have as part of your job. There are many good references for developing a standard business plan. However, when anticipating a looming recession, you need to have other elements in your plan. Do you have a plan of how the company would be restructured during a foreseen recession? Do you then have a plan on what you will look like when you emerge from a recession? How are you handling such things as layoffs and cost cutting?

Do you have a Business Plan "B"? That's a business plan and budget for the reduced income period and a plan of how the company will be structured when the recession is all over. The latter is very important since, many times, severe cuts are made during the downturn that dramatically reshape what the company can do when the recession is over. Key people are lost and important programs are abandoned in the name of cost cutting. Under these difficult circumstances, company morale can be seriously impacted. Rumors of plant closings, layoffs and major cutbacks can spread rapidly through the workforce – even when unfounded. Management must anticipate these situations and not allow them to go unanswered. How are you going to handle the layoffs? Are the layoffs going to be permanent? In other words, is the company going to permanently downsize?

    We all make the three- or five-year business plan showing our company's growth when times are good. Rarely does such a plan forecast a downturn where sales and profits will be dramatically reduced; owners and stockholders don't want that scenario from management. However, once a recession has begun, management must make a new plan that anticipates the next two years with *declining* sales and profits. The new plan must identify the new sales forecast. Typical recessions can result in a sales decline from 20% to 40% in capital-spending-dependent industries. Similar declines can be felt in other parts of the economy. At the very least, the revised plan must show a breakeven result during this period. Why two years? The typical U.S. recession lasts at least 18 months, so management must plan for the very worst.

    First, identify the key product sales that the company can focus on during the downturn. If you sell hardware in a business-to-business market, spare parts can be an important part of those sales. Spare parts' pricing should have margins of at least two to three times that of the basic products. Customers will always need some parts to keep the older machinery operational during the downturn.

Second, include more emphasis on service contracts if your company has a service department. Again, your business customers are also likely to be cutting back on their own maintenance departments with the idea of outsourcing this business. Make sure you communicate this service availability to those customers. Service pricing should be carefully calculated to cover all costs and show profits.

Obviously, the new plan cuts all discretionary costs proportional to the reduced sales forecast. Travel expenses are always a key target, but be sure to allow enough expense to provide contact with your key customers. Carefully review the staffing and what each overhead individual does. You will find redundancies if you haven't reorganized in a while. This will provide keys to staff cuts. When I took over as president of a small corporation and I interviewed all the key people in the management group, I found out that almost everyone had some sort of purchasing authority, which struck me as being wasteful. For example, the shop superintendent was ordering raw materials and consumable supplies for the shop, and office personnel had their own accounts with various other suppliers. No one was leveraging the ability of the company to purchase from given suppliers. We consolidated that function within a single purchasing agent that was the only one to have authority to purchase material for the company.

R&D spending must be carefully reduced. The company needs to identify any key projects under development and pick the one or two that can be completed in time for the next recovery. Having a brand-new product available for the market when the economy recovers can be a very important step. Protect the spending on that project.

One of the major responsibilities for a manager is to determine the business climate for the coming year and how it will impact the company's sales. The basics of a working business plan are a projection of sales. This information is gleaned from your district sales offices and key customers. But, as a manager, you must temper these details against the background business climate.

How do you really measure that climate as it pertains to your industry? If your industry has a trade association, that group might track your industry trends, which may be helpful in forecasting future activity. The purchasing managers' index can also be very helpful. When the index falls below 50, it is an indication of a future slowdown in economic activity. If your business sells to major markets, such as automotive or steel, they have indices that can be useful in projecting the future. At our business meetings, when we looked at sales projections, we also looked at all the various industry data that was available to help us glean not only the course of the coming years but also where specific marketing efforts might work.

If your analysis foresees a business slowdown, this can be a difficult projection to sell when everyone expects more growth. Unless you have a particular target market in sight that will mitigate these events, sales projections for the next year aren't likely to grow over the current year. As managers, though, one of your key jobs is to find those opportunities and move into them as quickly as you can. Putting a detailed plan in place to take care of the management of your core business activities will free your time to exploit these new opportunities.

Once your core business plan has identified the most likely base sales figures, be sure you have in place the management reporting tools that will keep you informed as to how that plan unfolds over the coming year. One of those tools is gross profit margin. Managing gross profit margin is important because all of your manufacturing and sales costs have been accounted for before you get to the gross profit line on the profit and loss statement. Set margin percentages for all your key products, including spare parts, with a periodic reporting system in place. Very competitive products with low margins should be off-set with high margins for key new products. The total margin must be high enough to cover your General and Administrative (G&A) operating costs. These are the activities you can manage that can impact your final operating results. These G&A usually include engineering, R&D, and marketing budgets, which can be leveraged to obtain maximum results.

One key activity to manage in any business plan is new product development. When any new product is first proposed, there should be a target selling price based on the market research that was fundamental to the original launch. Watch the projected manufacturing cost estimates as the R&D progresses. Any new product introduced must have a higher margin after costs than any existing products. Otherwise, why bother? Total manufacturing and distribution costs are now being wedged between the target sales price and the new higher margin requirement.

My experience is that the manufacturing cost estimates will increase as the development program discovers new problems that must be overcome with design changes. You will be forced to define whether the margin or the selling price will yield to these costs. Most likely, the margin will be the victim. This will be a bad compromise for your future profitability should this product succeed. It is very difficult to raise the selling price of a new product after it has been successfully launched, so you may be saddled with that low margin longer than you want. Attack those manufacturing cost estimates early to avoid that compromise.

In addition to purging non-profitable products from the line, sales increases can be obtained when new markets are developed. Sometimes, those markets can be in developing countries. This is a program that senior management should lead. Using the experience of your senior managers in developing these markets is key to the success of the effort. You will need to develop separate business plans and budgets for these efforts that have the complete support of the management.

Perhaps you see an emerging situation in one of the developing countries. There are many paths for entering these markets if you have not already done so. As an example, I can give you my own experiences in entering the market in China.

We began looking at China in the year 2000. At that time, the market in China had been open to the West for more than ten years. Some companies were in that market even before the opening to the West, but it was still not too late for new entrants if you had key technology that had a proven track record in Western markets. The Chinese technologists are very conversant with the successful technologies of the West and were then very receptive to their introduction in their own markets. Today, new technologies that reduce air and water pollution could be readily accepted in China.

Besides opening new markets, your business plan should include a number of other considerations in looking forward to the coming years. Cost reductions and cost controls are always keys to ongoing success. Too often, cost reduction is thought of as something we always do so we give it little specific attention. In these days of competitive pricing, that has to change. To get the maximum from your efforts, you need to make it a specific operational plan designating specific products and goals. A plan of reducing costs by 3% per year should be an achievable goal.

Purchasing activity can be a major opportunity for cost reductions. Purchasing is a critical function in your organization and has to be controlled at the highest levels. I discussed the company where purchasing authority is dispersed throughout the organization, where many different departments have purchasing authority. That will not give management control over costs. Centralize your purchasing, and give it management authority. A purchasing strategy with key suppliers is as important as a sales strategy.

Cost control is also essential. If you don't have a good cost reporting system for every product manufactured, be sure you include that in your planning. Out-of-control costs must be contained immediately. Every day lost can never be reclaimed.

Product pricing, as an integral component of your marketing plan, must be done at the highest levels. Too often, it is left at a low level. Pricing is a marketing strategy – not a sales strategy – and, therefore, a management task. All price decreases are subtracted directly from profits. Conversely, all price increases go directly to profits.

Layoffs and cutbacks take a toll on your company morale. Put into your plan activities that will help improve the motivation of your people. Plans that will help motivate everyone to achieve higher performance must be an integral part of your plans, even in difficult times. Make sure that the improved results can be monitored so that you can give credit to those responsible.

Identify and reward your high potential people. One of your key jobs as a manager is to either find these people in your organization and bring them forward or hire them from the outside. If you have shortages of these people, your plan must identify locating them and getting them on board. Many very good people get caught up in the high unemployment wave during a recession or company downsizing. It is your job to find them.

Form a small group of key managers and line workers to come up with cost saving ideas. Give them a target, and watch them exceed those cost-cutting objectives. The workers know where the waste is located. Trust them. Your trust will be rewarded now and over the longer term. Be sure to take action on many of their recommendations lest they think their efforts were not taken seriously.

Don't forget to hit suppliers for deeper discounts. Your suppliers also need to keep their order books as full as possible. Now is also a great time to re-look at the product line. There are undoubtedly older products with poor margins and declining sales. Get rid of them from the catalog. Fire sale the leftover inventory.

Look carefully at those weak sales offices. Marginal sales personnel need to be looked at carefully. Are they ever going to make the grade? Now is the time to make the hard decisions and cuts. Also, put strict limits on sales expenses for entertaining, shows and excess travel.

Only by updating old equipment and processes can you hope to keep ahead of the competition. You must identify specific plans for capital expenditures that will result in fast paybacks from increased profits. Your investment in capital projects must be at least equal to your depreciation rate. In good times, it should exceed that rate.

There are a number of ways to determine the future value of a current expenditure. One way is to calculate the value of an asset at any given time relative to its purchased cost as a function of the life of the equipment and the current interest rate.

A = Asset value at any given time
P = Purchase cost, use $100,000
n = number of useful years, use 5
i = yearly interest rate, use 3%

$$A/P = i(1+i)^n/[(1+i)^n-1] = 1.125$$

This means that the asset value each year of its life is more than the present worth at that time, a good result. If the interest rate increases to say 8%, then the A/P value drops to 0.25, not a good return. At 8%, the ratio is > 1.0 if the useful life is only one year.

The final part of our business plan must be a contingency plan. How do you hold your performance level if the general economic conditions deteriorate? How might new government spending impact your plans – both positively and negatively? How might they impact your customers? Your product offerings? Do interest rate projections play a role? How about the possibility of inflation or deflation? Does the strength of the dollar impact your exports or imports? If you foresee either significant increases or decreases in sales volume, how will this be handled? Is there enough plant capacity? How and when will layoffs occur? Or conversely, how will you find the people you will need for any major increase?

If significant changes are anticipated, it might be difficult to generate a business plan for the next two or three years. However, you must do it. It is just as important that the concepts you use as the basis for the actual budgets be clearly defined so that adjustments can be made when you know how those concepts and judgments fair as the year unfolds. That is when your contingency planning will pay dividends.

It's Called "Eating Your Seed Corn"

I volunteered for a time with a group called SCORE, which operates under the Small Business Administration. Its mission is to "…provide professional guidance and information, accessible to all, to maximize the success of America's existing and emerging small businesses." I spent some time counseling a couple that had been operating a private ambulance/transport service for about four years. It grew from a one-man service, generating $25,000 in revenue the first year, to a business employing 26 people with revenue of $785,000 in 2009. However, in 2010, expenses had gone up, the owners didn't think they would make any money that year, and they were having problems with their accounts payable.

It was an S-Corp business, and it had an $80,000 line of credit with a local bank, which was currently tapped out. The company owned five ambulances and three wheelchair vans. Dealing with hospitals and Medicare meant its accounts receivable ran at 120 days. That is very slow, but with these types of accounts, there is little danger of defaults.

A good corporate balance sheet that details the company's assets and liabilities is key to knowing how well the business is doing. Of course, being a small family-owned business, the owners didn't have a balance sheet! But that is something that their banker should have asked for long ago, because the way they were headed, the loan was at great risk as well.

So, what's the problem? It didn't take very many questions before we discovered that their vehicle maintenance costs were going through the roof. They didn't work on a budget either, so this came as an unexpected cost. For tax purposes, they claimed vehicle depreciation each year as a cost of doing business. However, vehicle depreciation is not a real expense, so the extra revenue that showed in their personal tax return became income. Their vehicles had become 100% depreciated. All had more than 200,000 miles on them, and some were approaching 300,000 miles. Breakdowns were very frequent and expensive. One vehicle broke down on a job more than 100 miles from home and had to be towed back. They had been eating their seed corn!

The solution we proposed was a very tight budget going forward, which had to include financing for at least two new vehicles a year, either through purchase or lease. They would need to do this quickly before they started having credit problems, which were just around the corner. To generate the extra income that would be required, they also had to include a marketing program beyond their current word-of-mouth business generation. This was something they had to undertake themselves since they couldn't afford any new employees.

Permanent Layoffs and Furloughs

When facing a downturn in business, the cost of labor will be a major factor. The new business plan must obviously address the cost of labor, both direct and indirect. Once the basic plan has been outlined, the money allocated for labor will be apparent. Management then needs to address the company personnel with an outline of what the impact will be. The first item to put on hold is obviously any planned pay increases and promotions. Perhaps the employees need to absorb a higher percentage of their health costs. There may be employees near retirement, and early retirement options can be offered. Identify those employees from your staffing review who will be given a permanent layoff.

Any permanent plant or division closings that have been identified in the plan need to be detailed with the timeline for these events clearly outlined.

Does the company have a well-defined termination policy in the company handbook? Surprisingly, many smaller companies don't have an up-to-date policy. Be sure you have a clear policy on what an employee given a permanent layoff is entitled to. It is typical to provide one or two weeks of pay for every year of employment.

Handle all the permanent layoffs on the same day. What's the best day? In my own experience, Mondays are best. That clears the air early in the week and gives the remaining employees the rest of the week to adjust to the impact. Fridays, I think, are the worst. It casts a pall over the following weekend without the time for the remaining people to discuss the consequences on their departments. It's also tough on the laid-off worker.

Don't hand out the "pink slips"! Managers need to talk individually to all those being permanently let go. It's the right thing to do. It is hard to do, but people deserve that one courtesy. Have all of their paychecks and other information from Human Resources ready to give them at the exit interview. It is best to have a witness with you at this time so there can be no unfounded repercussions. Answer any questions they may have about what they may take with them and other issues. Have clear company guidelines for this.

Don't walk them out the door through the department with a box in their hands! That is too demeaning. Give them some time to part with the friends they have made in the department. That goes for shop and office personnel. Obviously, in the shop, schedules must be maintained, so disruptions have to be minimized. Have the meeting in the morning, and let them leave by lunch time. Some may storm out immediately – so be it. Remember, memories of this day will linger, and one never knows what the next bend in the road will bring.

Temporary layoffs, sometimes called furloughs, are a very good way of controlling costs with minimal disruption to the longer-term goals of the company. Even before the layoff, employees are urged to take vacations. This can be particularly useful for direct labor personnel when shop orders are low. Some companies cut back on the hours per week with corresponding pay reductions. Another method is to give employees furloughs for one week at a time. After the first week of layoff, the employee is then entitled to collect unemployment pay for every subsequent week.

Furloughs need to apply to *every* employee from the top officer on down. This spreads the cost reduction over the entire company and will keep the employees' morale up knowing that the bosses are being hit just as hard. Cutting the pay of the top income people one week a month for a couple of months will reduce costs dramatically.

Not too surprisingly, it is my experience that the key office people will come to work most of the time during their furlough weeks. But it also gives them time to take with the family or other personal needs – particularly during the summer months. This approach is particularly valuable for smaller companies looking for temporary deep cuts in overhead that won't cripple the company over the long term.

This program is part of the plan that should be discussed with all the employees ahead of time. People know when times are tough. Major job losses are reported daily in the press, so they will welcome a frank discussion from management and a plan that protects their jobs/company over the longer haul.

Times of crisis are great opportunities to reflect on what you do and how you do it. During good times, everyone is busy keeping up with demand to spend too much time rethinking the organization. Harder times are when the chief operating officer should carefully review everyone's responsibility with the idea of reorganizing functions to save money. The excess organizational structure that has grown up during the good times will become obvious. The candidates for permanent layoffs will emerge from this study.

Employees older than 40 years are protected from arbitrary layoffs by The Federal Age Discrimination Act. The act also regulates things like job assignments, training, and promotions. The act applies to every company with more than 20 employees. Therefore, a permanent layoff or reassignment of these employees must be well considered to avoid possible legal implications. Older employees with their market and product knowledge can be the most valuable asset the company owns. Targeting older employees strictly for cost reduction could prove to be a costly decision. One mustn't look only at cost and benefits in evaluating people. If you have a well-documented case of a person not performing his or her duties, one can make a case for job termination. However, if that is the case, the employee probably should have been terminated before the cost reductions became necessary.

This is now where senior management's total review of the organization and the functions of the key employees will become important. Many times, this review will identify an older manager who is no longer doing a real job for the company. This might be the manager who has turned over his work to a subordinate and has failed to use his experience to identify other options. Basically, he appears to be doing his job, but the reality is that one of the subordinates is really carrying the load. Surprisingly, senior management may be unaware of this situation, but other employees are usually quite aware. This is where your careful interview will be useful.

According to an article in *The Wall Street Journal* by Jennifer Levitz and Philip Shishkin, the EEOC typically issues "merit findings" on about 20% of complaints. That means a negotiated settlement. In 2007, the EEOC obtained over $100 million in settlements. Another 60% are given a "right-to-sue" stamp, and the plaintiffs are free to file civil action. That will also most likely mean a settlement. Only 20% of the cases are dismissed. Not very good odds. Obviously, the best approach is to constantly engage your senior staff so you know who is not carrying his or her load. Then, a well-documented performance report will provide a more appropriate ground for a termination.

After you have made all the cuts in staff and budgets to match the reduced sales volume, what else should management be doing? The most important activity should be focusing on increasing sales. Management people, particularly those involved in the technical side of the business, can be a valuable resource in this capacity. Senior tech people visiting with key customers to review their current needs and focusing on how your company can meet those needs can be very rewarding.

The reduced activities at the plant provide more time for developing new ideas. Make sure you keep focused on the agreed-to new product development so that it stays focused on an early release when the recession is over. But what of other opportunities?

How are your competitors fairing? Is there an opportunity here for developing merger or acquisition plans? Some companies will be hit harder than others by the recession, and this will likely open the door to these discussions. Don't skimp on travel expenses for this activity. During the 1981 recession, during an overseas trip, I was able to develop a new relationship with a foreign producer to sell its products in the U.S. market on very favorable terms. This gave us a whole new product line to introduce after the recession and eventually led to a major realignment of our companies.

How about making a major upgrade to your IT systems? With business slow, some good deals can be developed. During the 2001 recession, following the great Y2K effort by the IT companies, we were able to get a very good break for updating our systems and installed a complete SAP management software.

If you are not using your experience as a senior manager to develop new ideas, why are you more valuable to the company than one of those bright younger managers (who are also cheaper)? This is why you get the "big money." Managers not engaging in these efforts should be the target of review for job changes.

Straight Talk on Federal Income Taxes

Finally, let's discuss the impact of federal income taxes on the economy. As businessmen and women, we all recognize the impact that federal tax rates have on our business planning and investment. It is very hard for me to believe that these representatives of ours can participate in this discussion in face of the most overwhelming evidence that lower tax rates encourage more investment and a larger GDP and more revenue to the treasury as a result.

The data is available to anyone who takes the time to investigate. The Brooking Institute publishes this data on its website. The first hard evidence was the Kennedy tax cuts in 1963. In 1963, the top marginal rate was 91%. By 1966, the top rate had been reduced to 70%. Between 1963 and 1966, revenue to the Treasury had increased from $160.6 billion to $130.8 billion, a 22.7% increase. At the same time, the revenue as a percent of GDP went from 17.8% to 17.3% - virtually no change.

Next came the Reagan tax cuts in 1981. The 70% top rate was reduced to 50%. From 1981 to

49

1983, the revenue increased from $599.3 billion to $808.4 billion, an astounding 34.9% increase! As a percent of GDP, the range went from 19.6% in 1981 to 17.5% in 1983. The GDP had grown so fast that even the higher rate of tax collection ended up as a lesser percent of the GDP.

The top rates were further reduced to 38.5% in 1987 and 28% in 1989 as part of the phased Reagan cuts. In 1987, revenue was $854.3 billion. By 1989, it was $991.1 billion, another 16% increase; whereas, the percent of GDP was unchanged at 18.4%.

Between 1991 and 1993, the tax rate was raised back to 31 and then 39.6%. Revenue did increase during this period, which was free of any recession from $1,055 billion in 1991 to $1,154.3 billion in 1993, a 9.4% increase over those three years, basically inflation. It is important to note that the percent of GDP remained in the range 17.8 to 17.5%.

Then came the Bush phased tax cuts from 2001 to 2003 where the rates went from 39.6 to 39.1 to 38.6 and finally to 35% in 2003. In 2003, revenue was $1,782.3 billion and went to $2,153.6 billion in 2005, a 20.8% increase. As a percent of GDP, the range, once again, was 16.2 to 17.3%.

The most obvious result of these studies from the year 1960 to the present is that the revenue to the Treasury as a percent of the GDP varies very little around the 17 to 18% – regardless of the tax rate. However, since that revenue increases dramatically at the lower tax rates, the GDP expands.

How can anything be clearer to those bumpkins in Washington – both Democrats and Republicans – when they continuously blame tax revenues for the deficits and play class warfare pitting the rich against the middle class. The poor and lower middle class in this country actually pay no tax, so it is silly to include them in this drama all aimed at our Representative's own re-election prospects.

One wonders if there is any hope whatsoever.

Chapter 3.
Understanding Financial Statements

In this chapter, I will discuss an area with which many engineers and technical people are not that familiar – the company's financial statements. When you are first promoted into management from the technical side of the business, you begin to see monthly financial results. At first, it seems quite straight forward when you see the monthly profit or loss statements. But do you really understand what is behind the numbers? Probably not, unless you have had some prior training.

Accountants have a whole series of different reports that show the financial health of a company. As part of the senior management team, you should know what these numbers tell you so you can more adequately plan the future of your company. You can't just leave it to the accountants to tell you what you should do as things change. As a manager, you are held accountable for being competent and honest. The accountant provides management with a score card, and auditing ensures that the score card is correct. The CEO or president must make decisions for the company based on this report as one of his key inputs.

In Chapter 2, I discussed how you make your business plan each year to allocate expenses and revenue projections such that you will show a profit for the year. Each month, you will usually see a statement called the "income statement" or profit and loss report, showing how the company has performed compared to the plan.

In addition to the income statement, the accountants will prepare a "balance sheet" and a "cash flow" statement. These are not so easy to read or understand. Many will put these aside once they have seen the results of the income statement. However, profit or loss is not as hard fast a number as you may think. The real position of the company can be hidden when observed from only the income statement. It's in the balance sheet that the real picture will emerge.

In this section, I will look at the financial reports of a fictitious company called "Acme Products" to see how it did during the years 2007 and 2008 as that great recession took hold. We will be using a 2008 year-end audit of Acme to analyze the numbers.

Acme Products, Audit for 2007 and 2008

The first thing I will look at is the income statement. The revenue is in thousands of dollars, so the income for 2008 is $33 million. You will also notice that there is a decrease in revenue of $7 million from 2007, a 17.5% drop.

	2008	2007
Revenue	33,000	40,000

Cost of Goods		
Material	9,900	11,500
Labor	6,900	8,000
Overhead	4,000	4,800
	20,800	24,300
Gross Profit	12,200	15,700

    For this company, the cost of the manufactured products is divided into the cost of the material used, the direct labor required, and the manufacturing overhead. These figures will not reflect the actual money spent for all of the material and labor for the year. These are the costs accrued against the goods sold for that year. Manufacturing overhead reporting will vary from company to company. For Acme, overhead includes the cost of unapplied time, manufacturing supervision, warehousing and freight costs, and any engineering costs directly expensed against the shop.

    It is useful to put percentages of the various cost items against the revenue figure. When we do this, we see that the material costs are 28.7% of revenue for 2007 and 30% for 2008, labor goes from 20% to 20.9% in 2008, and overhead goes up to 12.1% from 12 % in 2007. These increases are not unusual for a recession year. The gross profit margin drops from 39.2% to 37% of revenue.

    Next let's look at the other half of the income statement, expenses and profit.

Expenses	2008	2007
Sales	1,500	2,000
G&A	2,000	2,200
R&D	500	800
Depreciation	2,000	1,000
	6,000	6,000
EBIT	6,200	9,700
Interest	200	0
Taxes	3,100	4,850
Net Income	2,900	4,850
Dividend	2,000	1,700

On the expense side, we have the cost of sales, general and administrative (G&A), R&D and depreciation. These are the budget items controlled by each department during the year. The sales department did an excellent job of reducing costs 25%. Administrative costs were reduced by only 10%, while R&D took a big hit of 37.5%. Hopefully, that one big project to keep running is still being funded at these reduced levels.

And Acme managed to make a profit both years. In 2007, its earnings before interest and taxes (EBIT) were a respectable 12.1% of sales. Even in the down year, the company has earned 8.8% of sales. I wonder if Acme is spending enough on future products (R&D) to maintain this return? The company also picked up some interest payments in 2008, which I'll look at later.

You can also see that owners have taken most of the profits in dividends in 2008. Low R&D expenses and big dividends – is there something we should know about the future of Acme? These are certainly the types of questions you should be asking as a manager of this company.

Acme Products, the Balance Sheet

The balance sheet is a description of the owners' equity in the company. The basic form is Assets = Liabilities + Owners' Equity. Assets are the investments made in land, equipment, buildings, and inventory in order to operate. The liabilities and owners' equity reflect how those assets are being financed. All transactions are reflected on both sides of the statement, and only transactions measurable in dollars are recorded.

Now let's look at the asset side of Acme's balance sheet for the years 2008 and 2007.

	2008	2007
Current Assets		
Cash	1,000	1,000
Accounts Receivable	5,000	6,500
Less Allowance	(850)	(900)
Inventory	16,725	18,500
	21,875	25,100
Long Term Assets		
Land	14,000	14,000
Buildings	7,000	7,000
Machinery	30,000	20,000
Accumulated Depreciation	(11,000)	(10,000)
	40,000	31,000
TOTAL CURRENT ASSETS	61,875	56,100

First, we see that assets are divided into two categories, current and long term. Looking first at the current assets, we see that Acme ended each year with $1 million in the bank. The Account

Receivable has dropped 25% with the 17% drop in sales revenue. The allowance is for uncollectible debt. No matter how well we screen our accounts, there will always be circumstances where a number of accounts will have to go into collection, and some will never be recovered. In a down economy, this will be even more likely.

Along with a decrease in sales, Acme has reduced inventory but by only 9.6% compared to the 17% drop in sales. When a downturn first hits, it is not uncommon for the required inventory adjustments to catch up. But inventory must be reduced. The cost of goods in the 2008 inventory is about 63% of the sales revenue (20,800/33,000). The $16.725 million in inventory in 2008 represents future sales of about $26.5 million or more than 80% of the sales for 2008 (16.725/0.63). What is the company projecting for 2009? Inventory for Acme is way too high. It has far too much cash tied up in inventory, and with a possible long recession looming, this could be a serious problem as this inventory ages and perhaps becomes obsolete or unusable. Companies will sometimes continue to make inventory as the economy drops in order to keep direct labor employed. However, this cannot continue indefinitely.

On the long-term side, Acme has added $10 million in new machinery. We will see how that was financed on the Liabilities side. All land, buildings and machinery is depreciated over set schedules of time. In this case, in 2007, Acme had depreciated about 25% of its assets. With the addition of the new machinery, it is now

59

depreciating about 22%. This $10 million investment would be an unusual investment. Generally, one tries to invest each year an amount equal to that year's depreciation.

Acme Products, Balance Sheet Liabilities

This is the Liabilities and Owners' Equity half of this report.

	2008	2007
Accounts Payable	6,950	5,300
Note Payable	7,000	0
Accrued Expenses	8,025	8,800
	21,975	14,100
Long Term Liability	0	0
Stockholders' Equity		
Stock	38,000	38,000
Retained Earnings	1,900	4,000
TOT LIAB & EQUITY	61,875	56,100

On the first line, we see the Accounts Payable. This is the money Acme owes to its suppliers. It increases in 2008 by 31%, even as sales decreased. When this happens, we are basically borrowing money, usually with no interest, from our suppliers by not paying them on time. This is one way a cash-strapped company can continue to finance its operations if it can't get any bank credit. It is also one way by which Acme helped finance its increased inventory for 2008. Fortunately, it has good customers and an aggressive collection department since we've seen how Receivables has decreased. In addition, Acme also borrowed $7 million to purchase the $10 million machinery. The accrued expenses are usually salaries owed (such as accrued vacation benefits), taxes not yet paid and other bills that have been put on the books unpaid. Acme has no long-term debt, such as a mortgage.

The stockholders have paid in capital of $38 million. Because Acme is a privately held company, there are no regular stock purchases or sales. Note at the bottom that the total Liabilities on page 66 must exactly "balance" the total in Assets on page 64. The retained earnings are what cash is left after the dividends were paid. In effect, Acme took $3 million in cash plus the $7 million in notes to pay for the new machinery. Its retained earnings in 2008 reflect this plus the paid-out dividends.

So, let's review what we learned about these reports from Acme's 2008 year-end report. First of all, the income statement:

1. The basic form is Revenue – Expenses = Net Income.
2. Some expenses, such as depreciation, are not cash. Some expenses, such as cost of goods

sold, may not be actual expenses for the period reported. Those costs are the values accrued against the actual goods sold.
3. Owners' withdrawals (dividends) are not operating expenses but are distributions from net income.
4. Profit is how cash is internally generated to pay for new investments in buildings and equipment and to reward the investors. Profit is a necessary cost of continuing to do business.

Now let's review what we found on the balance sheet:

1. The basic form is Assets = Liabilities + Owners' Equity.
2. Assets are the investments made to operate the business, such as building, machinery and inventory. Liabilities and owners' equity is how those assets are financed.
3. The balance sheet summarizes the financial position at a given time, such as month end or year end.
4. Every transaction is an exchange. Every liability must be offset with an asset for the company to be an ongoing operation.
5. Only transactions measurable in dollars are recorded.
6. Profits increase owners' equity, and cash withdrawals decrease owners' equity.

As we continue our analysis of Acme's financial reporting for the years 2007 and 2008, we will next look at the most critical element in determining the health of the organization – cash flow. Previously, we looked at the income statement and the balance sheet. Even though sales dropped some 17% in 2008 from 2007, Acme made a profit on sales of $6.2 million before taxes in 2008 compared to $9.7 million in 2007. In the last two years, owners have taken $3.7 million in dividends, and in 2008, Acme invested $10 million in new equipment. All of this looks quite good, but how has Acme's cash position emerged? Facing another recession year in 2009 and possibly 2010, if sales continue to decline, will Acme have enough cash to cover perhaps potential losses in the next two years?

Cash Flow = Current Assets – Current Liabilities. Negative cash flow means a company is decreasing its available resources. From the balance sheet, we can construct cash flows for both the years 2007 and 2008, as well as the net change in capital over these two years.

	2008	2007
CASH FLOW		
Current Assets	21,875	25,100
Current Liabilities	(21,975)	(14,100)
Net Capital	(100)	11,000

CHANGE		
Cash	0	
Accounts Receivable	(1,500)	
Allow	50	
Inventory	(1,775)	
Acct Payable	(1,650)	
Notes	(7,000)	
Accrued Expenses	775	
Net Change in Capital	(11,100)	

From the chart on page 69, in 2007, we see that Acme had a net increase in capital of $11 million but a decrease of $100,000 in 2008. The total change over these two years is a negative $11.1 million in cash flow.

Let's look at where these changes occurred by looking at all the individual changes that occurred in the current assets and liabilities. There was no change in the cash on hand, which was $1 million at the end of each year. The accounts receivable has decreased $1.5 million. This is understandable as a direct result of the decrease in sales volume. The allowance for uncollectible debt has decreased $50,000, which is to the positive side of cash flow.

64

Accounts payable, a liability, has increased $1.65 million. Acme is falling behind in paying its suppliers in this recession and is using its suppliers as a bank for interest-free money. That will not likely continue before it begins to have delivery problems.

The inventory decrease was $1.775 million, indicative of the fact that Acme has that much less goods available for sale.

In purchasing that new equipment, Acme took out a short-term note of $7 million, which now shows up as an additional liability. The company has paid interest in 2008 on that note but has yet to pay on the principal.

Accrued expenses have decreased $775,000 mostly due to reduced taxes. The net shows the total decrease in cash flow of the $11.1 million.

Obviously, this sort of change in available cash cannot be sustained another year since, if you recall from the balance sheet, Acme now has only $1.9 million in retained earnings. Management has done a good job of containing the downturn through 2008 but must continue to show profits through the recession if it continues.

I have reviewed this simplified financial report from a non-accountant's perspective. I have tried to point out the key items a non-financial manager needs to know about in order to better understand his company's performance. The financial manager is not usually responsible for how the company gets its products and sales. His duty is to report on how well you execute these activities for the owners and shareholders. Understanding this instrument is important for everyone in management. A complete financial report may well have many other details about which I have omitted discussion.

At year end, this financial data would have been part of the auditor's report for the year end 2008. The auditor is usually an outside accounting firm hired by the company to review its own accounting procedures. The auditor's report follows a standard format. The first paragraph says *what the auditor did,* namely, that the auditor has examined the books of Acme by following generally accepted auditing standards, which include tests (rather than 100% examination) of the accounting records. These tests might include sample inventory counts to confirm company reports and review of accounts receivable. I've known of struggling companies that have loaded up the receivables to provide a better balance sheet. We will discuss this more in Chapter 6.

The second paragraph gives the *auditor's opinion*, based on the audit examinations performed. The key words in the opinion paragraph are "presented fairly" and "in conformity with generally accepted accounting procedures applied in a consistent basis."

Additional paragraphs with words such as "subject to" or "except for" are used when the auditor has found deviations from these practices. These are red flags that need to be paid attention. CEO's will fiercely fight the auditor over these additional paragraphs as they will not be well received by investors or banks. The leverage that the company may have over retaining that auditing firm has been known to occasionally impact the auditor's report. Accounting firms have been sued and lost over improperly reported financial results.

Private companies in which all the shareholders are the managers may not generate audited financial reports if they have no bank borrowing. Obviously, these may not be as reliable as an audited report. Owner/managers have been known to keep a separate set of books that more honestly reflect the status of the company from the one they may show others.

Next, I will examine a number of financial ratios to measure the health of Acme. First, I will look at short-term solvency. A company must have sufficient cash resources to stay in business. Liquidity means survival, and insufficient liquidity means bankruptcy. The short-term solvency of a company can be measured using some financial ratios. The *current ratio* is total current assets divided by total current liabilities. A current ratio of >1.0 is needed for a margin of safety. At year end 2008, Acme's current ratio was 21,875/21,975 = 0.995. That's marginal.

The next ratio we look at is turnover of assets. This is the *accounts receivable turnover*. This is the total sales/accounts receivable, assuming all sales are on credit. For the year 2008, 33,000/5,000 = 6.6, which means that receivables are "turning over" on the average of 6.6 times per year. This can be expressed in *days* by dividing 365 by 6.6, or 55 days. This is ok if our terms are 60 days but not so good if they are 30 days.

Receivables, unlike good wine, do not age well. The longer they go out, the more likely they are to be uncollectible.

Inventory turn is the cost of goods sold/inventory. Inventories are carried on the balance sheet at cost. For Acme, the ratio is 20,800/16,725 = 1.24. Dividing that into 365 shows that the company has 293 days of inventory! This should be totally unacceptable. This is a serious red flag as to Acme's short-term liquidity and must be addressed immediately.

The *account payable turnover* = cost of goods sold/accounts payable. This ratio indicates how well Acme is paying its suppliers and for 2008 is 20,800/6,950 = 3.0 times per year, or converted into days is 120 days. How many suppliers are going to keep Acme as a customer with that performance? From this, the company also is going to get a very bad credit rating.

As we have seen when we looked at the cash flow, there are significant short-term liquidity problems with Acme even though it has been making a wonderful profit every year! As I said when we began this exercise, reported "profit" is definitely NOT the whole story. When we look at Acme's cash flow and short-term liquidity, the results are not good. Even though Acme has shown an excellent profit on sales over the last two years in the midst of a 17% drop in sales during the recession, it is in serious short-term danger.

The good news is that Acme has no long-term debt to worry about. A measure of a company's long-term solvency is the *long-term debt/long-term debt plus equity* ratio. In this case, it is zero. The stockholders' equity in this company is $38 million so Acme can look for some long-term debt structure to help ease the short-term liquidity it has gotten itself into. Taking out a mortgage on its buildings and land currently valued at $21 million would ease the short-term problems.

For their $38 million investment, the stockholders are getting a dividend of 5.3% in 2008.

The biggest problem with Acme, like many manufacturing concerns, is inventory control. During the turndown in orders, Acme kept the shop busy making parts for inventory instead of doing layoffs. If the company was saddled with debt, this could have been a fatal decision because it wouldn't likely have access to additional capital. The company must also address the situation with its vendors as vendor delivery is most likely already a problem.

This exercise shows us why, as managers, we must look beyond the monthly income statement if we want to really understand what is happening in our company. Just because we show a profit doesn't necessarily mean that all is well.

Chapter 4.
Managing Marketing and Sales

In Chapter 1, I spent time discussing the management of an engineering department. As a young project design engineer with a BS and an MS in engineering, I never envisioned having direct responsibility for both marketing and sales in a company with a large national sales force and numerous international sales representatives. Yet, that is exactly where I found myself after about twenty years. At the time, I thought marketing and sales were two words that described the same thing. They are not.

Many managers, however, use these words interchangeably so that the necessary distinctions are lost. That is a big mistake. As managers, we must understand that these are two very separate concepts that are at the very foundation of how we manage our businesses.

There are many key elements of managing a business, but there is one that I've learned to hold as the most important: *The purpose of a business is to create and keep customers.* And the corollary to that is this: *A business must produce goods and services that people want.* The words *create* and *keep* can be stand-ins for the words marketing and sales.

First of all, let's talk about marketing. People buy products to solve problems. They buy expectations, not things. At its heart, a product is a group of perceived benefits and expectations that has value from the viewpoint of the buyer. It includes both the tangible and the intangible benefits that the customer receives when he buys. Thus, the way a product or service is presented becomes a very part of the product itself.

In its simplest terms, marketing is the way a company defines the design and the value of its products and differentiates itself from the competition. Defining those design values and differentiations is one of the key roles of senior management. Communicating those values and how we differentiate ourselves from the others is the role of the marketing people in our organization, for example, the advertising group.

Marketing is the basic method by which we create customers. Therefore, the marketing philosophy must be at the heart of our strategic planning. Many times, it is in the form of a mission statement or guiding principles. In truth, a customer is an asset that is more precious than any tangible asset on the balance sheet. Senior management must never get so lost in the "numbers" that it loses sight of the fact that one of its key roles is to *create* customers.

Now let's look at the role of sales. I define sales as the management and nurturing of the relationship between the company and its customers. Managing that relationship is never easy. Years ago, I found an anonymous ode to a salesman, the source has since been lost (The term includes women, who have become an important and growing element in the world of business-to-business sales).

Some highlights:

"A salesman is a quota to the factory, an overlooked expense account to the auditor, a bookkeeping item called 'cost of sales' to the treasurer, a smile and a wisecrack to the receptionist, and a purveyor of flattery to the buyer.

"He [she] must have stamina to sell all day, entertain all evening, drive all night to the next town, and be on the job fresh at 9 AM.

"He [she] wishes his merchandise was better, his prices were lower, his territory smaller, his goods more promptly delivered, his boss more sympathetic, his advertising more effective, and his customers more human.

"He [she] is absolutely certain that tomorrow will be better, that there is nothing he would rather do, nobody she would rather be, than a salesman."

  That is what it takes to bring our human side into our relationships with our customers. Those who do this well are proud to be called salesmen and are probably confused when they are described as "marketing representatives."
  I have learned that the best sales success is one that is controlled by the knowledge the salesman has about the customer and that is built on personal relationships and trust. To maintain that trust, the salesman must be the owner of that

relationship. A customer wants to see a single face that represents your company's products and services. I found this to be as true in China as it is in Pennsylvania. It is awfully hard to achieve this if you present the customer with a continuous stream of different faces from the home office.

I've known a salesman (unfortunately a competitor) that was often called into a customer's board of directors' meetings to discuss new capital projects that involved his products. Guess who gets the job! We had a very large customer whose plants had no receptionists (quite common these days) and access to the plant was gained only through security locks. My salesman for that account was deemed so valuable to the engineers planning new projects that the company gave him a security pass so he could enter any area at any time he was visiting the plant to discuss any current technology. Another of my salesmen became such close friends with a plant superintendent that he helped the superintendent move to a new house and was best man at his wedding! Those are relationships.

One of the most successful and often copied sales strategies is the protected geographic sales territory. This was an innovation of NCR Corporation early in the 20th century. It was taken to new levels by Thomas J. Watson, who took the concept with him from NCR to IBM. The impact of this concept is to increase the frequency and quality of a salesman's contact with the customer. The result is an accumulation of knowledge about the customer's needs leading to loyalty that keeps the competitors at bay.

Today, with the increased cost of travel and the reduced budgets, we are in danger of losing this contact. There is still no substitute for face-to-face contact with the customer. This must also include periodic visits to key customers from key members of the senior management team. In the words of James Champy, managers need to "…get out where the real world of business lies – in the marketplace."

The need for senior management to be out there with the key managers of your customers is true all over the world. If you have sales in other countries, key personnel must periodically visit with key customers there as well. Doing so will also give you the opportunity to evaluate the relationship between your direct sales person and the key customer personnel. These visits will help you better understand the culture in those countries, which may help you improve your products for that market. Also, remember that it costs something like ten times more to find a new customer than it costs to maintain an existing one.

While you are visiting with those accounts, look for ways your company can work with them on new ideas and products. Look for ways you can provide more education about the industry and your products.

Remember when visiting an account with your sales personnel that they are the key holder of the relationship. Do not insert yourself into that role as it will only subvert your salesman's credibility. Mostly, be a listener. However, direct the conversation to uncover any problems in the relationship and ways you can impact the relationship from the home office.

There is no business without customers for its products or services. Customers cannot be developed without some sort of sales effort. A lone consultant must organize his or her time to devote a significant amount of that time to developing new accounts – selling. The larger the corporation, the better organized the sales effort becomes. Even in very difficult times, your sales organization must continue to be active. Customers will remember who calls on them when times are bad as well as when everyone has money to spend.

So, who makes a successful sales person? Sometime ago, I participated in a seminar on successful sales techniques. By answering a number of specific questions, participants were categorized generally into three personality types – hunters, gatherers and farmers. The hunter is the usual prototype for the sales personality, the person who charges into a difficult situation and will never take no for an answer. In general, this is true. However, many customers, particularly many technical people who have purchasing authority, are farmers. These might be engineers who spend their entire careers involved with things not people. A powerful hunter might be too intimidating for this farmer. A more comfortable relationship might emerge with one who has a gatherer's personality – one who is more moderate and accommodating.

Both hunters and gatherers can be effective salespeople, but farmer types generally will never make good salespeople. Sometimes, in the area of technical sales, we look for the engineer who has that technical expertise to be able to understand the technology. We figure teaching sales techniques will be easy compared to trying to teach the technology to a political science graduate. However, if that engineer hasn't got the personal skills to deal with the wide array of customer types – from general managers and purchasing agents to shop superintendents – he will fail as a salesman.

My own experience has convinced me that it is easier to teach the technical skills than to change the personality. A four-year bachelor's degree is not a necessary prerequisite for a successful salesperson. In many cases, it can be an impediment. Team sports participation is a particularly good background for a salesperson. Athletes develop a self-confidence and aggressiveness that can carry them through the tough days of the typical salesmen experiences, help them handle rejection and allow them to be persistent and disciplined (the hunter type). In all cases, the person must show an aggressive personality and be someone you should feel very comfortable with during the first moments of the job interview.

Good salespeople, even more so than most employees, are really motivated by money. The most successful programs involve paying commissions based on sales and shipments. Usually, there is also a base salary in addition to the commissions. Depending on the margins your products sell at, the commission-to-salary ratio will vary. High margin products should be sold with a high commission-to-salary ratio. Basically, these are the products you want to sell first, so pay accordingly.

Senior managers with technical expertise, as well as presidents and CEO's, need to make periodic sales calls on key customers. These calls should always be made with the local sales representatives. First of all, the salesperson has the knowledge of the customer that will be very useful during the visit, and it will give you the opportunity to spend time with those soldiers manning the outposts. Difficult times also can be very good times to make these visits.

We did business in the "north country" of upstate New York. Winter can be brutal with snow off the eastern side of Lake Ontario in the hundreds of inches per year. When a salesman and a senior manager show up between the months of November and February, everyone will remember them. These vendors, not the fair-weather types, will invariably get the business. It is similar when times are tough financially and travel budgets are being shaved.

During these visits, be sure that the local rep carries the agenda. You should set the agenda items you wish to cover ahead of time, but let your local rep show his authority to lead the discussion. Don't make him look unimportant. Otherwise, you may find out that that customer will never again take a final word from your sales rep and that you will become the receiver of many calls you don't really want to handle. If you have never been a direct salesman, as many of us have not, you will find many interesting sales techniques being employed by your local reps. You will also get a better idea of how your company is being portrayed out there.

At times, you will also get into a meeting where there is really no interest in your company's products. This is sometimes very hard to read, but it can save you a lot of wasted time if you can quickly ascertain this. I remember making such a call with a very senior salesman at a steel company with which we had done many projects. We thought there was a new big project that we could bid on. But after a very short time, knowing how that particular mill operated, he realized that all the key decision makers on such a project were not present at this meeting. After a very short time, he closed up his catalog demonstrating our products and suggested that the meeting was over. It seemed uncomfortable to me, but it was, in reality, a relief to those people who had been called out to attend the meeting when no senior decision maker was coming.

Chapter 5.
Developing New Products

New product development shouldn't be undertaken only during the good times. During a recessionary period, it can be very profitable to have new products available to the market when the economy has recovered. At that time, your customers will be looking for new ideas as well. So, let's review some of the keys to good and successful new product development.

One thing I rarely see as an important part of new product development is the need to manage change. Many new products are built upon the success of previous products in the company's line-up. Much of that work is mainly driven to add new and improved versions of older successful lines. This is important work, and we'll discuss it more after we look at another kind of product development, which adds a whole new dimension to your business and requires managing change.

Developing an entirely new line of products not currently manufactured is a much more risky undertaking, and it requires a management atmosphere that encourages risk taking and some associated failures. This might be the type of expense that is very hard to justify during a recession, but with reduced business activity, it may permit management to devote more time to a new direction for the company because such a change will require real management skills.

If this product is to be an entirely new offering, the first rule is to be sure the new product idea will fit into the company's overall strategic plan. Unless you are planning to go into an entirely new field of operation, the new product should be a strong compliment to the existing products and able to be marketed through the existing sales channels. It most likely will be an add-on product to supplement the current offerings and will have to compete with existing alternatives. If your new product is to be a new version of a product provided by a vendor and currently being re-sold, it must offer a whole new set of unique advantages over that current offering.

Next, you need to have a development engineer and product champion who has the required background to undertake the leadership role. Most likely, he will be new to your company, having come from a company that may already be in that or a related business. However, it is critical to understand that he cannot bring with him any proprietary information from that company.

Before you begin to define the product objectives, the new expert serving as the project manager should spend several weeks researching current technical journals and publications for the latest technology available for the basic engineering of the product. What new materials might be available that weren't around when current products in the field were designed? Is there new computer modeling pertinent to the operation that will give new insight into efficiencies? Chances are good that there are many new technologies available in the marketplace that can be applied to a new approach and that companies already making the product are not using.

Following that research, it is highly recommended that you discuss the potential development with your key customers to get their insights into their needs and expectations. This contact should be the first in a series that will be in place during the entire development project.

During this time, it is also recommended that you purchase some examples of the competitive products already in the marketplace. Be sure to examine any patents that cover the technology. Carefully examine how the competition is manufactured and, if possible, how it performs. If the items cannot reasonably be purchased, make visits to evaluate the performance in the field and get some customer feedback.

With all this information, it is now time to clearly define the objectives and operating parameters for the new product. These need to be carefully laid out to emphasize the specific advantages that this technology will have to achieve over the available products. These will become clear markers for the product development team. Success or failure will be measured by how these markers are achieved. It is also appropriate at this time to define the projected cost for manufacturing the product and the expected sales volume. What are the requirements for the export market? What permits will be required? The margin between the cost and selling price needs to be set greater than the existing margins for the current manufactured products.

After you have investigated the design and marketing aspects of the new project, it is time to examine the potential for requiring new manufacturing technology or machinery that will be required to bring this product to market. Do you have the potential shop capacity? Will you be manufacturing in U.S. or in metric dimensions and tolerances? Most of the world's developing markets don't want to deal with U.S.-dimensioned parts. Do you have the necessary in-house expertise for key elements? Will some of the technology be outsourced? If so, identify the key subs and plan on when to bring them into the program.

Does it still make sense to develop this new product? Ok, but this is just the beginning! Now, layout the entire development schedule with key objectives and milestones clearly defined. These milestones must also contain times when key go/no-go decisions will be made. Leave room in the schedule for the expected delays that will most assuredly occur. Original prototype manufacturing techniques will most likely not be the same as will be required for the final design. But the prototype tests will determine if the objectives can be met before an additional investment will be made in manufacturing technology. Be sure to set up tests for determining if new material or control technology can be relied upon for the performances required of it.

Once your new product development is well underway and all your early milestones have been successfully reached, this is a good time to apprize your selected customers about your progress. If your plans include patents, be sure to have any people outside your company who are given access to the technology sign non-disclosure agreements to protect your rights. Use their feedback to calibrate your progress.

This will also be the time when the manufacturing department will begin to evaluate how this product will be integrated into the plant's operation. Sometimes, changes will have to be made to well-accepted procedures that will require new thinking in the shop. Maybe new safety procedures, higher tolerances or other new technologies will be met with resistance. "We don't do things that way here" will sometimes be heard. At this time, management must find the key shop leaders who can champion the required changes and bring along the rest of the shop.

Like everything else in life, a new product-development plan will not go as planned. Key milestone dates will slip. What will be the impact on the schedule? Is this acceptable? Is the product introduction keyed to some outside event, such as a key international trade show? If so, how will adjustments be made to get back on schedule?

This is also the time when cost overruns will happen. Be sure to run cost checks on all key changes made to the original concepts to be sure you can reach the final cost objectives. Bring the manufacturing people into all the key meetings to get feedback on manufacturing procedures and costs. They can also be helpful in detecting improvements in design for manufacturing efficiencies. Sometimes, people with critical skills will become overburdened with other demands and will decide on their own which of their many projects is more important. This is where management must step in to make those critical decisions. At this time, I like to remember the words of Peter Drucker, who often extolled management to "feed your opportunities and starve your problems." Be sure that as a manager you keep your key critical-skills people focused on your opportunities.

Somewhere, usually about two thirds of the way through the development, a critical failure will occur that will determine the fate of the entire project. This failure may appear small or unimportant at the time, but you must successfully resolve this failure or drop the project altogether. To ignore its implications or provide a Band-Aid solution will invite a future catastrophe of greater proportion when the failure occurs in the field where hundreds of products will be involved. And do not doubt that it WILL occur again. Success with this new high-margin product will provide your company with new markets and sustainable growth for many years to come when executed properly.

While the development of new product lines that are not related to current production items offers the company the greatest opportunity for internal growth, most product development involves products closely aligned with the current offerings of the company to either expand or supplement those offerings. Unlike the development of a totally new product line, this type of development will usually be handled by the existing R&D staff people. But that alone will not guarantee a successful product development. Many of the keys we discussed previously will also apply to this type of project.

It is just as important to maintain close customer contact during these developments to ensure the resulting product will meet the demands of the market. Be sure that your marketing team has had input into the potential volume and targeted selling price so that there are no surprises at the end. Also, the development team must be totally committed to the project with a clear understanding of the goals. When you kick-off such a project, be sure that the project goals, including cost and performance requirements, are clearly defined. During the course of most projects, the team will be required to make trade-offs. Understanding the goals will make those decisions much easier.

Develop a plan highlighted with key milestones. Leave time in the schedule for unforeseen delays and problems. Watch your cost estimates for the final design closely. Remember, a new product addition must have better margins to warrant the effort.

Be sure that as a manager you keep the team focused on the project. Just as in any project, some people with key skills will have many other company obligations. Management must determine their priorities, not the individuals. As previously mentioned, Drucker's advice to "feed your opportunities and starve your problems" is not always easy to execute when problems appear in your "in box" (whatever that may be) nearly every day. As a successful manager, you cannot be tempted to manage from your in box or you will never accomplish anything new.

As with all R&D work, don't ignore small problems that occur in the development testing. If it occurs during your development, you can be sure it will be magnified tenfold when the product reaches the customers' more rigorous and unanticipated demands. And, as previously stated, continue to talk to your key customers. Bring them in to review and comment at key milestones. Be sure they also sign non-disclosure agreements at this time to avoid giving away your technology. Be sure your marketing people are brought along so they can properly promote the final product.

Involve your manufacturing staff members early in the process to provide their input on containing costs and improving manufacturing efficiencies. One of the scariest development processes I have seen is where the engineering development team members literally toss their final prototype "over the petition" to manufacturing and figure they've done their duty.

Engineering and manufacturing can also do the same to the salespeople. At one time, a company had what everyone began to call "the product of the month." With no thought to the impact on manufacturing schedules or marketing, engineering was literally putting out new and improved versions and modifications to the product line every month. This is a very expensive exercise, not only from the cost point of view but also in the confusion it sets up in the marketplace as to which products the company is actually supporting.

Product improvements should always be on the agenda but handled in a well-thought-out program that maintains shop efficiencies and provides an even marketing profile for your company. However, with the rapid pace of technological change in today's world, as a company, you must be prepared to confront the need for new product development that involves a higher risk and a well-thought-out strategic plan and management control.

Company Trade Secrets

As important as how you will develop your company's products is how you will protect the particular details of those products. Most of us work in companies that have methods for manufacturing products or processes that we have developed and that differentiate us from the competition. These may or may not include patents and copyrights. When these processes are not revealed in public disclosures, such as patents or copyrights, they are kept as company "Trade Secrets." The most famous of these is, of course, the formula for Coca Cola. The company has protected the formula from public disclosure for nearly 100 years by hiding it in a vault with only very limited access.

So how do you protect your trade secrets when access to the information is needed by numerous operating personnel in performance of the jobs? It is a critical management function to ensure the safety of this information. Competitors can reverse engineer nearly any product these days and produce an "almost" exact duplicate. However, your own development of the product probably found that a slight tolerance variation in one or two key elements of the design was the difference between success and failure. This is now your trade secret and needs to be protected.

Several years ago, we set up a sales representative in China. In China, copying products is a way of life without regard to contracts or normal business practices. Sure enough, within the first year of our contract, copies were being made. Fortunately, we found out about it through one of its employees and cancelled the contract. After setting up our own sales organization, we heard from one of our customers that one of our products was not working in a major process line and causing much damage. Upon investigation, we found that the product did not have our markings and was one of the counterfeit models. The forger had missed one of the key design features in the form of a key tolerance, which negated the proper operation.

So how do you protect that feature? Well, here's how not to. In the United States, we had a customer that hired one of my engineers in order to make our product for its own use. Over the course of the years in doing business with this customer, our engineering department had sent the customer outline sales drawings for its use in adapting the product to its equipment. These drawings were done in a CAD format. In such a format, layers of design details are overlaid upon each other to get the final assembly. The final assembly can be configured to omit the underlying details and show only the finished outside dimensions. Such a drawing can be used for sales purposes. However, if such a drawing without removing the underlying drawings is sent electronically, it can then be deconstructed to reveal all the underlying details, including the part with the very critical tolerance dimensions!

When we saw the company's finished product, we were shocked to see it was nearly an identical copy of our product. Our suspicions were aroused. A search of the former employee's computer revealed that he had downloaded many of the key drawings of our design to his laptop. We knew of no reason he had needed these, so we got an injunction from the courts to have the other company reveal what was on his computer in its building. Sure enough, our drawings showed up in its shop! Open and shut case, you'd figure.

We filed a lawsuit, which was then legally finagled to be heard as a jury trial in the company's district court – a very southern city. Our company was in the north. Shouldn't be a problem in the 21st century, you'd think. Our corporate lawyers were from "K" street in Washington, DC. The very best.

Without going into any of the gory details, a key defense presentation was a showing of our drawings sent to the customer by our engineering department deconstructed to show every detail of our design! The stolen drawings were a moot point – we had GIVEN them everything they needed. The jury members were all local, and one could sense they did not appreciate our big time Washington attorneys. After spending more than one million dollars and months of key personnel's time, we lost. Basically, we had not protected our own trade secrets.

A company needs to identify what its trade secrets truly are and have written guidelines on how these are to be protected. All employees who come into contact with these items need to be made aware of them, as well as the proper handling of these items. Trade secrets that can't be reproduced from reverse engineering are better than patents and cheaper. Once you have written a patent, you have revealed much of your technology, and all a copier has to do is figure out how to achieve all of your results using a slightly modified approach to avoid your patent. This is almost always possible unless your patent protects the very basic foundation of the technology. That is a hard thing to do in this day and age.

Chapter 6.
Dealing with Dishonesty

All dishonesty is bad. Some dishonesty needs to be dealt with by dismissal and even prosecution if laws have been broken. Some dishonesty should be dealt with through a reprimand and a second chance. Then there are offenses that are misdeeds for which warnings will be issued. Usually, dismissal will follow after one verbal and one written warning about the same offense.

Your company handbook should be very clear about the types of dishonesty that will lead to immediate dismissal. New employees should sign off on receipt of this information. Activities leading to immediate dismissal might include improper use of company equipment, bringing illegal substances into the workplace, fighting with or threatening another co-worker, or violation of specific high-danger safety codes.

If you have hard hat, safety glass, or safety shoe requirements in certain areas, leaders must not violate these rules since others will follow that example. There should be no exceptions.

At the same time, making too many onerous conditions for workers to prevent minor theft can add a lot of cost to your operations. In the assembly area of our shop, all hardware was specified in the engineering drawing. The assembly mechanic would go to the local supplier with a detailed list of the nuts, bolts and screws he needed for the project. What a time waster that was! Besides the trip, there was the idle chatter with the attendant about the latest scores or fishing adventure.

As president, I recognized this problem, and we discussed providing on-the-floor bin control for all the standard hardware items used in assembly. But one concern was that people were going to just help themselves to these items for their home workshops. I convinced the managers that once they'd taken the few items they wanted, it would end, and the cost would be minimal compared to the lost time under the old system. So, the on-the-floor bin control system was installed, and it worked far better than expected. We no longer even tracked these items. The supplier did all the tracking and replenished the bins as needed. And there was the added benefit of reduced assembly time and cost for all the products. We did not encourage employees to take this material, and most probably did not, but in this case, allowing for a small amount of "dishonesty" resulted in a win-win situation for both the company and the employees.

Some employee dishonesty will never be a win for your company. When hiring a new employee, we all try very hard to run background checks and interviews to determine the veracity of the applicant and his ability to fit into our culture and do the job. Contacting former employees usually yields only an acknowledgement that the applicant actually worked for them – nothing about why or how they left. That's how our legal system works. Here's a story about hiring a sales manager from a competitor who had an outstanding resume that seemed to check out. He was also someone known by our organization as a competent competitor. Sounds good.

One of our requirements for employment was that he relocate to operate out of our home office, which was more than one thousand miles from his current home. Another request was that my wife and I meet with his wife at some time to help with questions about the relocation. We set up a date, but when that date approached, we were informed that she had had an accident when starting the trip and had to return home. Several weeks later, I was told that they had found a place on their own in a city about twenty five miles from our headquarters, with apologies that they hadn't called while in town. OK, we thought that we'd get together after they moved.

In the meantime, my new sales manager was traveling a lot to visit with our customers and salespeople. He submitted weekly expense reports, including lots of airline flights, which I approved with little review. They seemed reasonable on the surface. Then, small discrepancies began to surface about his whereabouts when visiting with our field people. When I got a call that he had failed to appear at a very important meeting, I got suspicious of all these unexplained events. We had still not met his wife after many weeks of employment.

I finally pulled all his expenses reports to see if I had missed something. I noticed then that up until the previous week, all his trips included a routing through his "former" hometown. A call to his home confirmed that the family was still there and that "daddy was on a trip." We were being taken. He was obviously using us to expense his costs in setting up his own business, probably the reason he was no longer with his former employer. When I called him in for a meeting to discuss and terminate, I never got to the end. In the middle of the meeting, he just got up and walked out without a word. I hope you never have such an experience.

Expense accounts are important tools for managing your business – don't take them lightly. Commonly, there are the padded expense reports taking advantage of loose control over expense report auditing. How many times have you been billed for an expensive dinner with a customer that was actually a private affair with no customers involved? Trade shows are wonderful places to use this to get around daily per diems for meals.

But there are more insidious white collar crimes that can be far more damaging to companies both large and small. If you are a small company with an outstanding loan from your bankers, you may have all your receivables routed through a lock box controlled by your bank. Under these arrangements, the bank will usually release funds to your account as you post new receivables from ongoing sales. One deception that will destroy your credit is to book "likely" orders in your account receivables to release cash from your lock box. How many times do "likely" orders turn into vapor? What do you suppose will happen to your relationship with your bank after this deception is discovered?

This deception, however, is not limited to lock box accounts. Some years ago, Bausch and Lomb, the giant optical company, was posting sales to its distributors without any orders from them for glasses. This gave a false projection of their sales for a given quarter, and the un-needed glasses were returned to the company the next quarter. Of course, this deception can only go on as long as there is a significant increase in real sales in a future quarter. Bausch and Lomb eventually had to restate a number of financial returns to the distress of its stockholders and eventually the CEO.

Many know the story of the accounting scandals at Enron. Here we had officers of the company setting up satellite entities in which to hide gigantic losses from the stockholders. Many companies have made some "slight" accounting changes in their quarterly reports to hide bad news from stockholders. These abuses usually start with the idea that managers will make up the losses in the next quarter and reverse the entries at that time. Many times, the situation only gets worse. In a public company, this can mean jail time for you if you are an officer.

The dishonesty that can really hurt your company can come from some of your most trusted employees. Stories of bookkeepers stealing thousands of dollars from small companies and not-for-profit organizations are rampant. In times of layoffs and salary cutbacks, we can expect even more of these incidents.

Dealing with Insubordination

The classical definition of insubordination in the workplace is an employee's willful disregard for a manager's direct order. However, when an employee steps outside of his or her authority to reveal a manager's actions or decisions to a non-qualified outside party, is that insubordination as well? Sometimes, that is called whistle blowing when the manager's action is clearly unethical or illegal. But what if that manager's action is perfectly upright and the employee's objective is to disrupt the plan?

I served on the board of a non-profit organization. An uproar was created when a member of the president's office staff discussed a possible operation that had yet to be approved with some outsiders who had vested interest in the area. The staffer was never told directly not to discuss the plan, but its confidential nature was well known. Without specific instructions, shouldn't the boss assume his staff will treat such details in confidence?

As a manager, how would you deal with this? In many instances, the guilty employee has previously exhibited indifferences to company rules and norms. The problem employee had been given "kid glove" treatment because the boss can't or won't face up to the inappropriate behavior. If this were the case, the real blame lays with the boss. This type of behavior needs to be nipped in the bud before such a serious transgression occurs. The rules for behavior need to be clear and enforceable.

Such an employee should never have been allowed to serve in such a sensitive position in the first place. For this case, the proper action is to address the problem once and done. Termination is most likely the best avenue.

But sometimes, a very loyal employee will get into a discussion where this information is inadvertently discussed or brought up with the hope that another course of action can be developed because the staffer sees a serious problem with the action. Of course, that employee should have rightly discussed it with his or her superior first. If you, as the boss, are not easily approachable, don't be too surprised when this happens, though. Under these circumstances, you may wish to pursue a different course of action, such as a severe reprimand after discussions with the employee.

Personal Integrity as a Manager

"Integrity without knowledge is weak and useless, and knowledge without integrity is dangerous and dreadful." Samuel Johnson.

What can we say when some of the best and brightest business leaders and politicians have failed us except that they have dangerously undermined our country. As business leaders, we must value our personal integrity as well as that of the companies we lead. Scandals involving politicians are always news. There have been so many politicians that have shown a complete lack of integrity that it has possibly undermined our faith in our representative government at all levels.

Dozens and dozens of state politicians have been sent to prison. If your state hasn't had them, either you are very fortunate or the corruption is so deep that no one has been able to penetrate it.

On a national level, the conduct of U.S. Rep. Anthony Weiner of New York, who sent sexually-explicit photos of himself to women, was preceded by that of U.S. Rep. Christopher Lee of New York, who resigned for his shirtless-photo incident. Before this, there were the problems of U.S. Rep. Charles Rangel, also of New York. As chairman of the House Ways and Means Committee – which writes the U.S. tax codes – Rangel allegedly didn't know he owed taxes on thousands of dollars in income.

In 2008, Gov. Eliot Spitzer of New York resigned for his escapades with prostitutes. A few years later, media reports revealed Gov. Arnold Schwarzenegger's ten-year lie about his own extra-marital affair. U.S. Sen. John Edwards of North Carolina ran for President telling a giant lie to all about his own affair and illegitimate child. Gov. Mark Sanford of South Carolina ran out on his marriage while concocting another lie to cover his affair.

Of course, we can go back to the notorious President Bill Clinton, who could have put the entire nation in jeopardy when he tried to cover up his own scandal. He, we know, was preceded by President Richard Nixon, who had his own troubles with integrity. Is there no shame?

Could your lack of integrity put your company or yourself in danger? How about that CFO for Enron, Andrew Fastow, who covered up millions of dollars in losses by hiding them off the books in phony subsidiary corporations? He was aided and abetted by his own boss, Kenneth Lay, who assured stockholders only months before the collapse that all was well with Enron. Lay died before beginning his eleven-year prison term. Fastow served six years. But the biggest fish with no integrity was Jeff Skilling, the CEO before Lay, who resigned and sold his $60 million in Enron stock. He was indicted for fraud and insider trading and is currently serving a 14-year prison sentence. Originally, he got 24 years.

I was a stockholder of Tyco International when Dennis Kozlowski was CEO. Kozlowski was convicted of misappropriating millions of dollars in company assets for his own benefit. He did so by conspiring with other officers to breach their own fiduciary responsibilities, offering them to share in his misappropriations. The company was nearly destroyed. As a stockholder, I lost thousands of dollars. Kozlowski served slightly more than eight years in prison.

Should we talk about Bernie Madoff? Madoff conned his best friends and business associates into the biggest Ponzi scheme of all times. You wonder what kind of thoughts go through the minds of these people as they fall deeper and deeper into that black hole of deceit and dishonesty.

How many more Weiner jokes will we have? What about that "blue dress"? What does the name Enron bring to mind? What about "I am not a crook"? "Reputation is what you do when others are watching. Character is what you do when no one is watching." I don't know who first said that, but it certainly rings true.

There are a couple more people that come to mind in these very troubled times. One of the worst U.S. recessions was set in motion in 2007 by the housing crisis that was the result of credit default swaps that no one really understood and that went into the tank. An officer at AIG Financial Products, Joseph Cassano, on December 5, 2007, stated: "We are highly confident that we will have no realized losses on the [company's credit default swaps] portfolios." In March 2008, only three months later, AIG posted a loss of $5.29 billion. How's that for the big lie! How could any CEO not see a $5 billion loss coming? For that slight oversight, Cassano was forced to retire in 2008. But he received $280 million in cash, $34 million in bonuses and a one million per month consulting fee so they wouldn't lose his 20 years of experience! Fortunately, the consulting fee was later dropped, but taxpayers forked over $85 billion to salvage the company. Last we knew, Cassano was hiding out in London.

Also aiding in the housing collapse were the two federal housing programs – Fannie May and Freddie Mac. Whatever these monstrous government bureaucracies do in this world, in the spring of 2008, then Chairman of the Federal

Reserve Ben Bernanke stated that these entities were in "no danger of failing"!

None of us is perfect. We all have our individual weaknesses and flaws. It's how we deal with those weaknesses that make for integrity. The little white lies, the forgotten golf strokes – small items in themselves – but if you let your guard down, they can lead you into the big lie that can crush your reputation and your company. America, we need to restore our sense of honesty and integrity. As America's business leaders, it can begin with us.

I recently read where Warren Buffett said that reputation takes twenty years to build and five minutes to ruin. The lives of some very prominent politicians and businessmen have been ruined. As an executive, you most likely consider your reputation to be your most important asset, more so than your technical competence. And why not? As a manufacturer, you have a reputation to uphold to your clients, your owners, and the people who pass judgment on you every day.

Any operation or senior manager within your company can impact your company's overall reputation both positively and negatively by individual actions or by corporate activities. As a company, you take risks in the marketplace regularly. Those risks must be monitored regularly to ensure you have not crossed the threshold of an activity that can destroy or impact negatively the company's reputation. When an individual's actions put the company in the negative media spotlight, as managers, you must take action immediately to distance those actions from your corporate reputation. That's easily done. But what do you do when your company's actions come under fire from the media?

Many of us never have that kind of contact with the media and so are very vulnerable to a media blitz that puts our company in a bad or unfavorable light. That media attention can make or break your company's reputation in a very short time, so you need to have a media plan in place before such an incident hits. That incident can come in many forms, such as an explosion or fire causing severe damages, a disgruntled worker causing mayhem on your premises, or a faulty product that went undetected and has now caused secondary damages.

You must have a plan for both the traditional media, as well as the social networks and blogospheres. The response must be pertinent to the problem – no contrived statements that sound like obfuscation. A poorly thought-out response may smack of a cover-up, and as we have seen in so many cases, the cover-up can become worse than the original offense. You may want to consider the purchase of media time to tell your side of the story if that is appropriate. Having your senior leadership out in front of your customers or public will be crucial in salvaging your company's reputation. The personal integrity of those individuals will also be tested under these conditions. Remember the story about Ken Lay of Enron and Joseph Cassano of AIG who got out in front of their companies' bad news with lies that destroyed both them and their companies' reputations.

Chapter 7.
Leadership in Times of Crisis

Management is always about leadership. During the more difficult times, your leadership can be crucial to the very survival of your company. Leadership is not about style. There's the George Patton style, as well as the Steve Jobs style. They all work if you stick to the basic principles.

In the tough times, you have to take actions that are going to be very unpopular, the results of which won't be known for years to come. You will be comfortable in those decisions if you know you are doing what is right and follow your own well-defined principles.

Keep your cool when confronted with seemingly endless troubles that pile on one after another. Some subordinates will make stupid errors. OK, once it's been done, the only real approach has to be "now what are you going to do to fix it?" There can be nothing worse in your organization than an atmosphere of total fear. People cannot perform properly when they have total fear from repercussions from the boss. Inherently, you already know this, but it is surprising how many managers don't recognize their contributions to this state of affairs.

Robert A. Kierlin, a co-founder, president, executive chairman, and CEO of Fastenal Co., wrote a book titled *The Power of Fastenal People*.

In it, he summarizes his David Letterman-style ten rules about leadership.

1. CHALLENGE rather than CONTROL
2. Treat everyone as your equal
3. Stay out of the spotlight
4. Share the rewards
5. LISTEN then SPEAK
6. See the unique humanness in all persons
7. Develop empathy
8. Suppress your ego
9. Let people learn
10. Remember how little you know

These can be very simple rules for life as well. How well can you follow that guideline? How many bosses have you had that ran that sort of operation? Most of us will have a few weaknesses that will fall outside of these principles, but the majority of good leaders probably will have most of these principles as part of their day-to-day dealings with their subordinates. Kierlin built a $400 million company around them.

During my early career, I had a string of some unusually bad bosses who had very little respect from their subordinates. My first job as an engineer at a giant aerospace company was under one of these. I had done quite a bit of research about a problem we were having with one of our products and wrote up a very detailed report on what I had found and a proposed solution. When my boss read it, he informed me that the report would be issued under his name. It was an important subject that was going to be circulated high in the organization. When I protested this revision, I was told that this is the way business works and that I had a lot to learn. That started my quest for a new job.

You must allow your subordinates their opportunities to make names for themselves. When you hire people that are smarter than you are, you prove perhaps that you may be smarter after all. You can consider yourself a good leader when you demand good work from your people.

Unfortunately, in my next job, I ran into a boss who was intimidated by my work. I did a major research project for a brand new product line that he had directed me to undertake. When I submitted my proposal for review, the math I included with my analysis was apparently way beyond his comprehension. After one evening of review, he gave it back to me with one note (in red ink no less) that stated the design would never work! No explanation was offered, and no discussion followed. Time for a new job search.

Again, let your people have the opportunity to try their ideas. Working with the opportunity or threat of failure is a great tempering process for one's development. Of course, you don't want or expect failure, so you need to guide them through the process using your own experiences as a guide post not as a directive.

Moving on, I once again ran into a take-all-the-credit type of boss. There are a lot of you guys out there. This time, it was over patents. If you've ever had the opportunity to submit an idea for a patent, you know that all patents are listed under the principal inventor's name. If there are more inventors, they become "et all" in any listings. When we submitted my designs for patents, my boss informed me that since he was the senior officer in the department, his name would be listed first, even though he had nothing whatsoever to do with the invention. That seemed strange, but I had no knowledge about patents until I was discussing some of the details with our attorney. That's when I learned that the principal inventor's name must, by law, be the first name. That was the beginning of the end of my relationship with that boss. However, he later was fired, and I became the new VP. Sometimes, there is justice.

    As senior managers in your companies, you may be called upon on short notice to deal with the local press or to manage a clean-up when an environmental accident by your company impacts your local neighborhood. I will refer to some personal incidents in which I was either involved or impacted by such an event.

    The first of these is the near catastrophic events of Wednesday, March 28, 1979, at the Three Mile Island nuclear plant in Middletown, PA, less than 10 miles from where I lived at the time. The management of this crisis eventually went all the way to President Jimmy Carter, who visited the site on Sunday, April 1, five days after the event. However, I want to discuss the role my next-door neighbor played in these events. This gentleman was a senior manager for the plant's owner, Metropolitan Edison.

To give you some background, we'll review a brief sequence of events of the accident as they happened. At 4 a.m. on the morning of Wednesday, March 28, operators doing some routine maintenance accidentally blocked the flow of cooling water to the reactor of unit 2. Within 10 seconds, a series of events took place that led to a significant release of radiation and a complete meltdown of the reactor core. By 9 a.m., the entire core had melted and had dropped to the bottom of the 5-inch thick steel containment vessel, which miraculously held. At 1:50 p.m., there was a hydrogen explosion, which was also contained by the containment vessel. Plant officials did not know specifically what had happened at this time; however, the media was generating a lot of misinformation, resulting in a general panic among the public that lasted until Sunday, April 1.

On Thursday, my neighbor was ordered to the plant as part of the crisis management team. As the senior officer at the site, he became the company's spokesman to the press. What happened after that caused a great deal of public distrust of his company and the entire nuclear power industry.

By Friday, two days after the accident, the episode had reached a national audience. Locally, schools had closed early, and the kids had been told to go directly home and close all the windows in their houses. The local population was becoming extremely nervous about the events at the plant. By Friday morning, already more than 48 hours into the accident, no official at the plant knew for sure what had happened. There were reports in the media of a potential hydrogen explosion in the reactor that would spew radiation all over central Pennsylvania. Of course, we later found out that the explosion had already happened and had been totally contained.

At 11 a.m. on Friday, this senior executive addressed the press corps on national TV. His role was obviously to assure the public that his company had the situation under control. He opened his statement by saying that only 300 millirems/hr of radiation had been released but was immediately challenged that over 1200 millirems/hr had already been reported. He became agitated and confrontational. I remember watching his press conference and thinking that he wasn't doing very well under the relentless questioning. Then, he said, "I don't know why we need to tell you each and every thing that we do specifically…" At that point, both Met Ed and my neighbor's credibility with the press was done. Later, on Friday, Harold Denton of the Nuclear Regulatory Commission took over the management of this crisis from Met Ed.

This situation was handled so badly that the entire nuclear power industry has been impacted. No new plant has been started in the United States since that day. The crisis management team assembled by Met Ed on Thursday failed to get its arms around what had happened and totally failed to convince the public that its officials could handle the crisis. Denton and his assembled team were able to do this and had the crisis cooled by Sunday. However, to this day, there are those that still don't believe the whole story was told.

Unfortunately, this manager did not prepare himself adequately on the events and their potential consequences to be able to calmly convey this to the public. His being thrust into this enormous event under these circumstances is not enviable at all.

How prepared are you? When you contract for the sale of an industrial building or land, the purchaser or bank will most likely want to conduct an environmental audit of the property to determine if any environmental liabilities exist. Regardless of who actually may have caused any contamination of the property, if environmental harm is found on the property or the property is found to be the cause of harm to adjacent properties, the current owner will be liable for the clean-up. Therefore, when purchasing an old property, the new owners will usually want to determine its environmental condition.

Old industrial properties located in areas called "brownfields" are most likely to have been environmentally contaminated over many years of use, particularly if that use extends over a century or more. That was the case with a property I was selling, located in upstate New York along what used to be the old Erie Canal. In fact, the property was located on Erie Boulevard in Syracuse.

The sale of the property was part of the sale of a company and was an integral part of paying off the bank loan. The purchaser of the property was going to convert the old industrial building to a new auto parts warehouse. The land had been part of the industrialization along the old canal for more than 150 years.

The buyer wanted to conduct an environmental audit of the land as part of his due diligence. The company conducting the audit was drilling core samples on the property when one of my older employees informed me that the drilling was about to occur in an area where he was sure there was an old abandoned oil tank that had never been removed. The new buyer was also present at the time.

When I received this information, I approached the buyer who was standing nearby and informed him that he was about to lose the opportunity to buy this property at the bargain price he had contracted for. The discovery of the oil tank would immediately halt the sale and require monitoring of the surrounding land for any additional spills from this tank. Then, there would be the enormous cost of the "clean-up" of property that had been contaminated for more than 100 years of industrial use. What else would they find?

A few minutes of discussion ended the environmental audit. The buyer had his building and the site for his new warehouse without further hassle. Up until this time, no harm had ever been attributed to the property and certainly no additional harm would come from the sale. All the surrounding properties were industrial use as well. An environmental crisis was averted. What would you have done if you were the buyer? The seller?

Old gasoline service stations that don't have new double-walled tanks and concrete retaining walls could be subject to leakage into the surrounding soil. That was the situation with a station located up the hill from my home. The way the situation was handled by officials should never be repeated.

There was some new development on the hill behind the gas station that required extending the sewer line from the development behind my house to the top of the hill behind the station. Coincidently, that same year, the gas company dug up the natural gas line running down the street in front of my house, which also ran past the station, to replace it with new pipe.

There was some heavy snow fall the following winter and a lot of rain the following spring. One spring night after a particularly heavy rain, the neighbors behind our property had to abandon their homes when they were overwhelmed by the smell of gasoline vapors.

The State Department of Environmental Conservation was called in to assess the problem. The old gas station was, of course, the immediate suspect, and tests on the property confirmed it as the most likely source of the contamination. Contractors were called in and began ripping up the land around the homes behind us to decontaminate the soil. Neighborhood meetings were held with the DEC engineers to give progress reports. For some reason, we had no gasoline odors in our house, but we were included as part of the probable contamination area.

The DEC engineers presented us with maps that showed a massive wave of gasoline spilling underground through the entire neighborhood. The thought of all this contamination seeping into every home caused much anxiety and panic. The DEC, in addition to excavating large tracts of soil, also began to drill monitoring wells throughout the neighborhood. At this time, we refused to permit the DEC any access to our property because we had no evidence of any contamination. I also didn't relish having our property torn apart at random, looking for the gasoline "wave" as was happening to our neighbors' properties.

As the summer wore on, we became the subject of attack by the DEC for hindering the solution of the problem by non-cooperation with the government. The DEC contamination map showed the probable contamination area well onto our property. We were now being shunned by our neighbors, who were living amidst mounds of mud and clay when the DEC identified us as a problem hindering the clean-up process. The contractors continued their attempts at abating the situation by digging more wells and trenches. Some of the neighbors had yet to return home.

The oil spill from the gas station on the top of the hill was now a serious problem. The state had now sniffed gasoline vapors running down the edge of my property along the street line – right along the line of the recent new natural gas line. They were positive that it had to be seeping across our property and that we would soon have it in our home. Our home was the oldest home in the area, having been built in 1812. No other home had previously occupied the land. There was a 200-plus-year-old pine tree on the property. Obviously, the land around our home had not been disturbed by man since the last ice age had come through upstate New York. It was inconceivable to me that the gas would be coming "through" that hard packed soil when so much development and new excavation had taken place all around us.

At the next neighborhood meeting, I presented to the DEC engineers the possibility that the gas was following the recent sewer line extension from the neighborhood past the gas station and that gasoline vapors had entered their homes through the laterals. The gas vapors found in front of my home had most likely come down the line of the recent natural gas pipe installation.

The engineers from the state knew nothing of these recent construction projects after several months of tearing up property and causing panic. It was now fall, and mounds of dirt had yet to be replaced in the property behind us. Following the meeting, neighbors who had been shunning us came over and admitted that I had been right in keeping the state off my property from the beginning. No gasoline had yet been found in all the soil torn up on their properties. The logic of my argument was becoming apparent to all.

The soil was all now being replaced in the yards, and monitoring wells were being placed around the area to determine how far the gasoline had spread. After serious negotiations, we finally let the DEC place a monitoring well in our yard, which never showed any sign of gasoline.

I was appointed spokesman for the neighborhood at this time. Our first order of business was to go to the town taxing authority. We all got a 30% reduction in our taxes due to our property being "contaminated" with gasoline for as long as the state kept monitoring wells on our property.

The engineers from the DEC had acted irresponsibly. If these engineers had not been from the state but from the oil company, civil lawsuits would have resulted. A lawsuit was, in fact, filed against the company that owned the station, which eventually settled with only a minor payout. Government DEC engineers, acting without restraint or regard for the citizens for whom they worked, caused much harm to both the citizens and their cause. As a private company, this arrogance over personal property rights would never have been permitted.

Chapter 8.
When Owners and Managers Fail

For the most part, the owners of America's businesses that aren't publicly traded are looking out for the long-term interests of their businesses. In that sense, they invest in their companies to ensure a long-term survival. Private owners, for the most part, know that sometimes they are competing in a world market and that their survival is dependent on their ability to compete on that stage with technology and competence.

But it is not universally true. In a global economy, some of these highly successful small U.S. businesses operating with a weak U.S. dollar have been bought up by foreign investors who see these companies as cash cows for their own enrichment. Today, the term for this is "globalization." These smaller companies probably have heavy investments in technology and facilities and a secure low competitive market for their unique products. As such, they have a vast storehouse of "seed corn" that can be liquidated by these new owners. Hopefully, your company is not one of them being bought out. But let's look at what could happen if your company is bought out by a large conglomerate and you survive the cut.

In the name of greater efficiency and high hurdles for investment decisions, these large conglomerates may slowly bleed the purchased U.S.-based companies of their huge stockpile of assets generated sometimes over many generations of workers and technologists. Depreciation of assets becomes an instant cash generator when no new investments are generated. Instead of reinvesting in their manufacturing base, they "outsource" large portions of their formerly in-house manufacturing base. In so doing, they also get a reduced cost from the elimination of the manufacturing support structure, which can now be "downsized." There is no more depreciation as a cost element, and the profits for the owner soar.

Outside vendors are now counted on to provide all the manufactured items from electrical control systems to machined sub-assemblies. Supposedly, this can continue indefinitely as long as there are subcontractors around, but can it?

With no in-house manufacturing capability and tightly controlled inventories, customer deliveries become at risk. Production schedules can't be adjusted in house to meet suddenly changed customer demands. Design engineering can no longer work with the production process engineering people, who no longer exist in house. Long term, that can become a significant detriment to good product design, but that assumes one is in it for the long term, which many of these investors are not.

Not to mention the impact of mother nature – snow storms, hurricanes, volcanic eruptions, and so on – on the ability of airlines and trucking to make on-time deliveries. As a result, a whole new division of labor has been generated called "Managing the Supply Chain."

When field problems arise, something that will always be with us, quick solutions can't be generated using in-house resources for making new parts or re-working complex control systems because the company no longer has control over these shop-type resources. Using the supply vendor for this work puts the situation in jeopardy to that vendor's own priorities for people and schedule.

I have an economist friend who says that outsourcing is the natural progression of manufacturing. He uses the analogy of the American farmer. Years ago, the farmer raised his own horses for work, saved his own seeds for planting and, in general, provided all the goods and services he needed to plant and harvest his crops. Today, another outsourced manufacturer provides the tractor and the seeds and the fertilizer. Harvesting may even be done using high-cost machinery rented from the local supplier of equipment. It's called focusing on your core business.

But is that the same analogy? I say it is not. The farmer had no need for any of the technologies needed to produce a tractor, and everyone used the same seeds and fertilizer. The farmer had no competitive edge using his own resources. That is not true about a competitive manufacturing company. The competitive edge is gained by how a product is produced as well as by what it does. Outsource and you will slowly lose any connection to how your product is produced and any advantages that could come from that technology.

Outsourcing manufacturing capability is a cost saving because it presumably permits the owners to focus on "core businesses." Does this completely assume that how you manufacture and how you service your customers with delivery schedules and correction of problems in the field is not part of your core business? Does that make any sense?

But in today's economy, it can be even worse. The next in-house capability to be "downsized" will likely be the R&D department. Previously, we have argued that an active R&D project is a key operation to be fully funded during a recession. Being able to introduce this new technology to your markets when a recession is over is an excellent way to jump start your own recovery and get a leg up on the competition.

We know that many of the products used, for instance, in the industrial markets have a working life of many decades before they are made obsolete by newer technology. If your plans don't look out that far, why spend money on projects that will take many months to develop and many more months, sometimes years, before the market will accept the technology if that is beyond your time horizon.

But you don't just eliminate the R&D group, as that would send a terrible message to the rest of the company. You pare its budget, and you present high hurdles for any proposed project to clear before funding is approved. The department putts along working on minor upgrades that give the illusion of a fully funded program. But it is deceptive if there is no long-term goal.

At some point in time, after all the savings can be taken from this outsourcing and downsizing, the leftover bones of the original company can also be sold off at a steeply discounted price. The new owners will integrate whatever technology is left from the remains, and another piece of our U.S.-based manufacturing is lost forever. This, in my opinion, is the result of globalization. The new owners and senior managers make a killing. The original company probably disappears along with the majority of the middle-class workers. The community suffers a severe loss of revenue and support for local projects.

Maybe from the perspective of maximizing your cash flow as an owner, all of this makes sense. But that imperative is not the goal that drove many of the entrepreneurs of U.S. industry. Some of their names are still part of this world, but the spirit that drove them to produce the technology that put the United States in the forefront of many industries is gone in many instances. This is particularly true with some of those companies that are now part of a big international conglomerate run by a bunch of numbers guys. Somehow, I don't think we are better off as a nation as a result of globalization.

Maybe we can acknowledge that outsourcing can result in generating additional cash for the owners, even if your company is not merged into a large conglomerate. In addition to the loss of what I deem to be a very key part of your core business, outsourcing has its own built in perils.

Supposedly, now the same manufactured parts can be brought in through that wonderful new technology called the "supply chain." Inventories are reduced with "just in time" deliveries. Subcontractors who become dependent on this new-found business can be pressed by purchasing agents to lower their prices. That's a lot easier and cheaper than coming up with innovative new ideas to lower costs. Purchasing agents are also a lot cheaper than skilled engineers and manufacturing technologists.

Of course, for the sake of costs, it is not uncommon that little time is spent with these subcontractors to ensure they have met the same standards previously imposed by engineering on the in-house manufacturing people. Instead, we rely on our in-house receiving quality control that can, at best, test for dimensional and material conformity.

In a perfect world, one could predict exactly what products his customers will buy and be able to order the correct volume of parts to process that need. Inventory costs plummet, deliveries are on time, and customer satisfaction soars. But in today's economy, anything but that is happening. In the real world, suppliers become insolvent, and snow storms and weather hamper ground transportation. Volcanic eruptions and terrorist threats can shut down air deliveries for days.

Managing these risks will now become a full-time job for a number of people. So what you have done is replace the traditional manufacturing managers with new risk managers. A new overhead is put in place to replace the old overhead you thought you could live without. Unless you have a perfect method for forecasting your customer needs, you have also given up control of your production scheduling to your vendors.

So, the message is, be very particular about how you define your core businesses. For many companies, manufacturing capability is, most likely, a vital element in that exercise. Outsourcing your payroll may be okay but your manufacturing capabilities? Be very careful.

Chapter 9.
The Impact of the New Technologies

Some call it the "baby-boom echo." The generation born between 1977 and 1996 is actually bigger than the boom generation, and it will dominate the 21st century, numbering more than two billion people worldwide. These people have grown up in the digital age and have been "bathed in bits." There are more people in this group who use the internet in China than in the United States. They are the collaboration generation because they have grown up interacting.

The internet makes life an ongoing collaboration, and the baby-boom echo generation loves it. They can sift through information at the speed of light by themselves or with their network of peers. MySpace and Facebook are among today's largest networking communities with more than one hundred million people hanging out there. Facebook was recently valued at more than $50 billion! For the Net Generation, according to the book *Wikinomics: How Mass Collaboration Changes Everything* by Tapscott and Williams, it is a private space in which they can invite a thousand friends.

The key point to this emergence is that it signals how today's Net Generation is predisposed to connect and collaborate with peers to achieve its goals. In the future, you will not be able to ignore the networks that these managers are forming. As workers, this generation will transform the workplace and the way business is conducted to an extent not seen since the 1950's. Eighty million people in the workforce will be a powerful force for new collaborations. They will also raise new challenges for employers trying to adapt to their new expectations. This generation will demand highly collaborative and collegial work environments. Companies that will adapt to this new demand will gain a tremendous advantage in competitiveness. But will they be able to innovate?

There is a new perfect storm of technology, demographics, and globalization developing. The result of this convergence will result in the change in the structure of the corporation itself as companies open up and collaborate with external resources. From a recent article by Theo Francis in the *Wall Street Journal*, in the late 70's, an employee was more likely to be working for a firm with fewer than 100 workers than one with 2,500. Today, a quarter of U.S. workers are employed in firms with at least 10,000 people. Between 1980 and 2014, the manufacturing sector lost 8.5 million jobs. Technology. Robots and artificial intelligence have certainly been a factor, but much U.S. manufacturing has also moved offshore with globalization.

In 1991, Ronald H. Coase received the Nobel Prize in Economic Sciences for his 1937 work "The Nature of the Firm." In this paper, according to Tapscott and Williams, he questions why individuals join together in companies rather than act as individual buyers and sellers. One of the main reasons he found had to do with the cost of information. Producing a product – from a loaf of bread to a car – requires the close cooperation and common purpose of workers. It is impractical to break down each process into a series of separately negotiated transactions. Each transaction would incur individual costs that would outweigh any savings.

First of all, there would be search costs to find appropriate material suppliers. Then, there would be the contracting costs and, finally, the coordination costs of meshing it all together. The corporations concluded that it made more sense to perform as many functions as possible in house, resulting in the emergence of the vertically integrated corporation. The result is that a corporation will thus expand as long as it is cheaper to keep an operation in house rather than going to the open market. Conversely, if it is cheaper to go to the marketplace, do not do it internally. But, again, are you outsourcing and losing control of a critical function?

There was an article a few years ago in *The Wall Street Journal* by Andy Kessler discussing how video games have supplanted the military in the development of some of our newest technologies. In that piece, he discusses how the Chinese announced they had created the world's fastest computer, clocking at 2,500 trillion operations per second powered by processors from Nvidia, a Silicon Valley company that developed these chips and sold hundreds of millions of them for video games!

What a change. Today's computers, along with so much of our current technologies, were first developed by the military for such uses as calculating artillery firing tables and breaking code. Just as a side note, I used my first vacuum tube-powered computer as an Army Artillery Officer, calculating trajectory tables for the Honest John nuclear missile in 1960.

Kessler refers to Apple's iPhone, which derives all of its technologies, such as color LCD displays, low power usage and precision manufacturing, from videogames. Videogames like Nintendo DS and Sony PSP sold in the tens of millions.

Now we read of machines being designed from molecules. The semi-conductor and computer hardware are a $1.5 trillion per year business. Three-dimensional printing will usher in a whole new age of manufacturing. This "printer" is not being used only for prototypes either. Regular manufactured parts are being generated. So how long is it going to be before you design your next product driven by tools that use these technologies? Where are you going to find the people who can do this?

Today, high scholars compete in a national robotics contest. I recently watched a telecast from St. Louis of the national contest. My grandson was the programmer for his high school robot. The robot had to identify a specific box, pick it up and deposit it in a bin. I think his team finished in third place. Amazing!

So how is this going to impact your factory of the future? The old monolithic multinational that creates value with a closed hierarchal management structure is on the way out. Success in today's world will require companies reaching out beyond their boundaries to use knowledge and technologies from other sources. This will apply to even the stodgiest of the industrial manufacturing companies if they are to provide the new products that will compete in the world's markets. But they probably won't, as they fight to protect their market share and profit margins. Your small innovative company using the newest technologies will most likely be the ones supplying the newest ideas.

Some of the mega companies are innovating. One example, taken from *Wikinomics: How Mass Collaboration Changes Everything*, is the new Boeing 787 *Dreamliner*. Boeing has staked a great deal of its future on this revolutionary technology, which has substituted new high-strength composites for aluminum in much of its structure. Boeing's giant plants in Everett, WA, and Charleston, SC, have become basically assembly plants for components that represent more than 70 percent of the airplane and that have been co-designed from scratch and complete subassemblies fabricated by more than 100 companies from six different countries. The original specification document sent to suppliers who were to design and build their component was only 20 pages long! But it has not been without its own unique problems either. The program fell about three years behind schedule and missed several rollout dates before it gained final acceptance. However, the technological advances promised in this design will likely set new standards for the industry. In the process, Boeing is going from an airplane manufacturer to a systems integrator. Maybe your company can be a supplier for this type of project.

In reading about how this phenomenon has been developing in world-class companies, I was surprised how far one of the most highly regarded car companies in the world has gone in this regard. BMW focuses on its core strengths of critical engineering, marketing and managing its partners. Its partners or suppliers make most of the components and increasingly manage the assembly of the final vehicle. It turns out that a company called Magna International can assemble a vehicle faster, cheaper, and with better quality than BMW itself. Today, innovation is shifting from mechanical engineering to digital electronics. BMW estimates that 90 percent of its new innovations will come from digital electronics, which it must consider as part of its core competence.

BMW and Boeing are not giving up on innovation by any stretch. They are using the resources that they have freed up to focus on new challenges. But this is nothing compared to another story from *Wikinomics* about the motorcycle industry in the city of Chongqing, China, a city of some 31 million people. In this smoggy, industrial city near the Yangtze River in Western China, the Lifan Group motorcycle company employs 9,000 workers and builds 700,000 bikes a year for customers in 112 countries. But it is how this was done that is particularly pertinent to this discussion.

The original designs for motorcycles in China were, of course, reverse-engineered from the Japanese designs. The Japanese should not have found this too surprising because much of their industry has a long history of reverse-engineering. But in Chongqing, several innovations made this a more collaborative project. The approach was to emphasize a modular motorcycle architecture that enables suppliers to attach subsystems to standardized interfaces. High-level designs set out the blueprints that allow suppliers to make changes to components without modifying the overall design. At every step, suppliers of adjacent parts take joint responsibility to ensure their components are compatible.

It sounds like chaos, but face-to-face relationships, which from my own experiences in China are crucial to all business activity, make it work. The result is that the modular architecture creates the opportunity for increased specialization, which drives innovation and improvements in quality and performance, keeping costs to a minimum. Chongqing assemblers build bikes for export to Asia that have dropped in price from $700 to $200, dropping Honda's share of the market from 90 percent to 30 percent. Sounds like Henry Ford and his Model T maybe?

But Lifan Group is also now in the automobile business as well. The Lifan 520 mid-size sedan is equipped with leather seats, dual air bags, a huge trunk, and a DVD system with a video screen facing the front passenger, all for $9,700.

Chapter 10.
What Might the Future Bring?

In *Drucker: The Man Who Invented the Corporate Society,* Peter Drucker is quoted as calling management "the most important innovation of the 20th century." The American century was driven by the successes of giant corporations, such as GM, Ford and IBM. Each of these giants developed a model for business that has impacted every company during this last century: Henry Ford, with his ideas of mass production and organizing the assembly floor; Alfred Sloan of GM, with his models for management structure and organization; and Thomas Watson, with his ideas on sales management at IBM. They were among the leading visionaries of the 20th century who helped create the managed corporation as the answer to the industrial age, which brought luxury to the masses. Much of what you do as a manager in your company comes from these models.

    Many of today's large corporations have become riddled with bureaucracies that include managers more concerned about self-preservation than responding to market forces. Maybe this is also present in your company. So, in fact, good managers become enemies of their own corporate structures. As a manager today, you must be prepared to confront new technologies, new communication technologies, competition from places previously never heard from and new government regulations making some of our technologies totally obsolete.

The advance of technology is so swift. I've read that it took radio 38 years to reach an audience of 50 million listeners. But television reached that in 13 years, the iPod in three years, and Facebook in two years. Changes in many industries are not quite that rapid, but all technologies have had enormous change over the last 35 years.

Since I entered the workforce in 1960, the 30 Dow Jones Industrial Average companies have totally changed. Only GE, Procter & Gamble and DuPont are still listed. Nearly 30 percent of those listed in 1960 are no longer even in business. Companies from the 1960 listing like Sears, AT&T, and Kodak are only shadows of themselves today.

The giant mainstay that practically invented modern photography, Kodak, has struggled enormously with extracting itself from the chemical business since the advent of digital photography. Then, there's Bethlehem Steel, once the supplier of steel to all the great 20th century construction projects and part of the great manufacturing engines that won WWII, now just a museum, put away with newer, cheaper steel-making technologies. And even one of the leaders in that early transformation, Motorola, today struggles with the newest innovations in mobile communications, having been outdone by newer start-ups with better ideas.

The leaders of these companies were not bad managers because they followed the 20th century dictates of "good management." They listened to their customers, they provided good returns to their stockholders, they studied the market trends, and they allocated capital to improve their performance, but they totally missed the step change in technology that drastically reduced costs or opened markets for blockbuster new products. Take a lesson from these giants. Don't let your company become a dinosaur.

When I graduated from college with a degree in aeronautical engineering, I first had to serve time in the Army after the ROTC commitment. This was in 1960. I had my commission as an artillery officer and was sent to Ft. Sill in Oklahoma for officers' basic school. Firing an artillery shell onto the correct target from thousands of meters away is a very mathematical operation involving trigonometry and very precise measurements and calculations. To accurately make those calculations, we used logarithms – five place tables – for multiplication and division. We also had very elaborate firing charts that gave powder and range specifics for each type of gun we fired.

After graduating from that program, I volunteered for an assignment at the school involving some new technology the Army was developing – the use of a computer to design the new firing charts for the Honest John rail-fired, nuclear-tipped rocket. (It sounded like a better position than going into a field unit). I had never even seen a computer after four years of engineering education, but I was now training as a computer programmer using machine language. This huge, vacuum-tube-powered machine (which it seemed burned out a tube almost daily) was basically being used to calculate multiple regression analysis from operational firings of the missiles in the field, from which a complete firing table would be generated. My hand-held HP calculator is probably 10,000 times more powerful than that machine of some 60 years ago. Talk about productivity!

Following the Army, I went to work at Pratt & Whitney Aircraft in East Hartford, CT. I worked in a new office building that housed some 3,000 engineers, all engaged in gas turbine design and development. When I entered the office complex on my floor (I recall there being some three floors), I counted the structural columns to arrive at the correct aisle where my work station was located and then counted rows to get to the correct place. Wow! Imagine hiring a new engineer into that environment today!

Then, I spent the next five years working on the 18 inches of engine that comprised the combustion chambers for the JT8 and JT8D engines. There were no combustion modeling or fluid dynamic modeling programs that could come anywhere close to describing the combustion process inside one of those six-inch-diameter combustion chambers. For calculations, we had our trusty slide rulers or, for more precise calculations, the Friden mechanical adding machines (that could also do square routes if you knew the correct manipulations). But precision calculations were hardly necessary since you had only a qualitative idea of what was going on inside that can in the first place. But by shear manpower and literally years of trial and error, P&WA built some highly reliable and successful gas turbines.

What was it like to manage in that era? The management of that "empire" was broken rigidly down into sections. Each area had an area supervisor, who took care of the administrative functions for his group, which might include members of several different product teams. Each product team of maybe eight engineers had a junior product engineer as its leader. His job was to be sure his group achieved the goals set out. Several of those junior product engineers reported to the senior project manager for that project, such as the JT8D engine program. Those project managers, in turn, reported to the chief engineer, who reported to the vice president of engineering. Quite a hierarchy – very formal to boot and probably like many other large engineering operations at that time – and very much like the military in structure.

After five years of this, I handed in my resignation. I must have made some sort of impact, because I was called into the chief engineer's office for an interview. His first question was, "Why are you leaving us?" The interview ended abruptly when I responded that "after five years, this was the first time I had even met my 'chief engineer.'" I guess he didn't like that answer.

From there, I went to a relatively small operation in the industrial heating business where a group of six engineers worked for the chief, who was also the VP. But even this was very formal and structured. Each engineer had his own area of expertise, and there was little if any cross communication between us. If you had a problem, you solved it with basically your own resources and what help you could wangle from the technicians in the lab, which was under the direction of one of the engineers. I guess the chief enjoyed the competition between us. But productivity improved when in the early 70's, we actually had access to a very large IBM 360 computer programmed in Fortran. The world of the slide rule was rapidly disappearing.

Of course, engineering productivity continued to increase with the IBM personal computer and the Apple Macintosh in the mid 80's. The IBM units, however, weren't nearly as useful as the Macs until the introduction of the first Windows program. Communications and coordination took an enormous leap in productivity when email and cell phones arrived. We purchased cell phones for my salespeople in the early 90's when they could become much more productive verifying appointment times without searching for a pay phone – particularly in upstate New York in the winter!

We can speculate on the future. Companies will have to be more agile and more attuned to a more competitive and dynamic marketplace coming from all corners of the world. Employees will form virtual teams for problem solving. There will be even more focus on customers and competitive strategies with leaner, less hierarchical management in structure and decision-making authority. There will be more team-based collaboration to provide all of the various new skills that will be required in developing new products and solving the new needs of the marketplace. Communication will be vital between team members, which may even include specialists that are outside of the corporation.

Changes in communication technologies have been revolutionary from the days of typewritten memos with multiple onionskin copies giving way almost overnight to email. Closely guarded company files can now be accessed by employees spending more time outside of the office with new smart phones and iPad technologies putting unprecedented power in the hands of individuals far from the home office.

Now, tools that may still confound many of the older generations are being used readily by the new generations. Blogs, chat rooms, peer-to-peer networks (Facebook, LinkedIn) and even personal broadcasting are allowing individuals to collaborate more productively. Employees can even act globally today, easily connecting with customers, suppliers and partners and adding value to the firm's ability to operate quickly. The Net Generation has grown up with these technologies as part of its birthright.

But smart companies are using social networks in many different ways. Set-up a Facebook account for your company, and through the many contacts generated, you can do market research for new products. Many companies now have official Twitter handles and Facebook pages for their brands. On these pages, the CEO and other top executives can join in the conversations personally, adding another level of contact.

Technical personnel can deal with customer techs in their LinkedIn accounts.

But there are also many possible negatives to be aware of when employing these networks. The Net Generation will want to bring their social networking life into the office and make it as much a part of their business life as it is their social life. Bringing the whole company onto a Facebook account requires a whole new set of policies. These activities cannot be centered in one single area or department. Perhaps you need to have a formal course for all those who want to participate in the social network to be sure you have a consistent message coming from the company. The ultimate objective of these exercises is to extend the company's ability to listen to your customers on a more informal arena.

Of course, you must also be very concerned about what exactly is shared on these networks. Some companies using these networks have opted to track everything that is posted to ensure compliance with company objectives and to make sure employees and sometimes agents don't do something that they shouldn't do. With a professional social-networking service, such as LinkedIn, the risk can be the loss of control over valuable sales files and contacts. Because the employee is by-passing your internal contact management system, the network becomes the employee's, not the company's.

Then, there are the iPads, CD's, thumb drives and other personal media libraries. These devices can store vast amounts of data. That data can also be proprietary and confidential but very easy to carry out the front door.

We haven't even touched on the impact of robots and artificial intelligence. Self-driving cars? Computers that aren't programmed but "learn" from experience. An article by Michael Milken and Igor Tulchinsky in the *Wall Street Journal* discusses the impact of technology on human capital. They suggest that "half of paid work can be automated with current technology." They suggest that "enlightened manufacturers are minimizing layoffs by preparing assembly line workers for higher-level duties." These are the new challenges you will face in this new environment.

The older generations, today's senior managers, have valued loyalty, seniority and authority in the corporation. The next generation (perhaps your generation), and the next millennial generation, it is said, reflect a desire for creativity, social connectivity, fun, freedom, speed, and diversity in the workplace. Your challenge as a manager will be the ability to attract and keep these new generations, who will be the leaders of tomorrow, while maintaining control over the company's customers and core competencies.

I can't pretend to be much of a forecaster of the future of how businesses will be structured, but I will rely on those people so presupposed to round out this discussion of being a manager. Much of the following discussion is taken from Tapscott and Williams. It seems appropriate to discuss some of these ideas to provide a window into what the future might look like for managers.

We previously discussed Coase's paper titled "The Nature of the Firm." In that study, as summarized by Tapscott and Williams, Coase describes how corporations were necessary for distributing the work effort efficiently and for protecting trade secrets. His prize was awarded at the very dawn of the Internet Age, which has changed everything. Now people on different continents and with different skills theoretically can work together on complex tasks without a large corporate structure. But is that really likely that individuals will be able to do this with the advent of the global corporation with tentacles in every national government?

However, this only reminds me once again of the old corporate guru Peter Drucker, whose most important advice for a manager was to "feed your opportunities and starve your successes," as stated in *Innovation and Entrepreneurship*. In fact, more than fifty years ago, Drucker had seen the corporation losing its legitimacy. Drucker held that the purpose of the corporation was "the creation of legitimate power." The power of managers grew out of "the property rights of the individual," making it legitimate power. However, as stockholders abdicated their rights to management, the corporation became independent, controlled by no one and responsible to no one. Now these global companies literally have their own foreign policies it seems. Globalization, perhaps, has even changed the very nature of the large corporation.

Interestingly, Drucker saw "the only solution [to the modern corporation] which makes possible both a free and functioning society is the development of the plant into a self-governing community." If only he could have seen the impact of the social networking made possible with the internet. Or maybe more independently owned and operated businesses – the small companies – that are the lifeblood of a free society will return.

Drucker, again in Tarrant's book, found much difficulty in the fact that the modern corporation had lost its legitimacy when the stockholders' by-proxy voting lost control over the management. To reclaim that legitimacy, management had to be responsible for "the economic interest of the enterprise and of society." The economic interest of the enterprise was, of course, profit. Profit is not a reward; it is the life support system of the enterprise. Not surprisingly, when discussing the role of the worker in this new order, Drucker's answer was the same. Everyone was to "see his job, his work and his product the way the manager sees them, that is, in relation to the work of the group and the product as a whole," as stated in *Innovation and Entrepreneurship*.

The modern shops that have work centers building entire products with teams of salaried equals is one step in this direction. One such company that I referred to previously is Nucor Steel. Each of its plants is an independent unit with full authority to manage its operations. Each department operates as a team, picking its own workers. Everyone shares monetarily in the production efficiencies.

Drucker, the eternal optimist, did have a positive outlook for the corporation. He continued to look on the organization as the framework within which a livable society could be built. What choice do we have? He maintained in *Innovation and Entrepreneurship* that we live in an industrial world. (Drucker wasn't a part of the "post-industrial society.") Moving into the future involves risk. To try to eliminate risk "is not only futile, it can be harmful. The bigger your job, the greater the risk you should be taking" as a manager.

Does this describe your company in today's world? It must be fairly apparent that the 21st century is going to usher in a new age for energy use. Taxes on emissions and carbon footprints are being discussed with more frequency. Global warming may or may not be a giant hoax to create a more controlled economy, but it does appear that it will have a major impact on our use of energy. You will have to deal with the consequences.

The changes that are coming will go to the heart of how we run and manage our businesses. As stated by Dave Garwood and Michael Bane in *Shifting Paradigms*, "A paradigm is a set of rules and regulations that 1) defines boundaries, and 2) tells you what to do to be successful within those boundaries." The old paradigm followed some basic truths with which we were very comfortable: The United States is a major supplier of heavy consumer and industrial products and basic materials; most automobiles are made in Detroit and run on cheap gasoline; coal powers 50 percent of U.S. electrical energy; the only atmospheric pollutants that manufacturers have to be concerned about are NOx and SO2; and maybe even that the United States is the land of free enterprise and entrepreneurial spirit.

The new paradigm could be that automobiles will only be assembled in the United States, the world economy could be heading for a longer-term depression, and the mighty U.S. dollar could lose its place as the world standard. Fossil fuels will be replaced with new technologies. CO2 emissions will have to be curtailed. Or the United States might reemerge as a manufacturing powerhouse and the world leader in energy production. The European Union may collapse. The Chinese economy might also collapse as have so many controlled economies in the past. Global warming may not be such a threat. Or, God forbid, a major war could break out.

What a range of uncertainty. How much of this really matters to your small business? As a senior manager, how are you preparing your company for this new era? Is your sales structure set-up to move into a world-wide distribution if you sell to heavy industry? How does the auto industry fit into your long-range plans? Have you planned on how to reduce your CO2 emissions? Do you have products that will help reduce CO2 emissions? Will that even be important?

As managers, we are constantly making decisions that bear on the future of our companies. A decision is basically a judgment. One tends to assume that decisions are based on facts, but that is rarely the case. In *Innovation and Entrepreneurship,* Drucker teaches us that decisions are based on conflicting opinions about conflicting alternatives. Opinions are like the scientific hypothesis. In science, one finds the validity of a hypothesis by testing it. So the question to ask is, what do we have to know to test these opinions? What will be the criteria for measuring the possible consequences of the various opinions? In management, this is not a mathematical calculation; it is risk judgment.

Drucker also points out that when there is consensus, there is no need for a decision. A decision is needed when there is disagreement. However, disagreement alone is not enough to provide alternatives for a decision. A decision without alternatives is a gamble. During the execution, you may find that the final decision is wrong. If you have gambled, the alternative is failure. If you have weighed alternatives, the alternatives examined will give you a fallback position.

So, to be an effective manager, make sure you have organized disagreement. You will never be able to lead your organization through rapidly changing times if you have surrounded yourself with only those who agree with you without question. When we made bold moves that were out of the norm for our company, one of my more conservative managers would question these decisions as being too radical. I told him that I was going to be right maybe 80 percent of the time and that we'd just bury the 20 percent of mistakes, so just get going. But his questions did serve as a check point.

Now the alternative to making a decision is "to just do nothing and maybe the problem will go away." This can actually be the best course of action if the problem is of little consequence and the alternatives will make little difference to the outcome. In many situations, if we don't act, we'll probably survive. But maybe by acting, the company will be far better off in the long run.

Act or don't act, but don't hedge or compromise. However, during the execution, listen to those inner demons or that questioning manager asking the tough questions. Nine times out of ten, they are probably of no concern, but the tenth time might be the one. When it is, act quickly to change course. As an executive, you are not paid for doing things you like to do. You are paid for getting the right things done – making effective decisions.

Appendix

During the year 2000, while developing our business plan for the next year, we discussed how new markets may be the key to growth. Specifically, we discussed the emerging markets of Brazil, India and China as fertile ground for introducing new technology.

We had received an email from a company in Nanjing that wanted to sell one of our key products in the Chinese market. As with a number of companies, in 2000, we had no representative in this fast-growing market. However, we did have an English-speaking representative in Taiwan that had some sales on the mainland. Our first inclination was to let this rep take over managing the possible account in Nanjing on a commission basis. So, I arranged a trip to China where I would meet him in Nanjing. He set up the visit with the principals of the new prospect and acted as my interpreter since neither of the two principals knew English very well, or so I thought.

During that first meeting, I was very impressed at how much knowledge they had about our company and the specific products they wanted to sell, and after a while, I realized they were quite fluent in English. The internet and our website was the key to their knowledge. China, I found out, has the largest number of users of the internet in the world. The principals had very detailed knowledge of the market they wanted to sell into since they were already selling other equipment into this market. We reached a contract agreement quite easily. They had an importer and a shipping company they worked with out of Shanghai, which at that time was the nearest port of entry. They would handle all the details on duties and fees; all we had to do was load their order in a 40-foot container and call the shipper. It couldn't get any easier.

Sales took off immediately after my return. However, trouble soon came about between our Taiwan rep and this new mainland company, as you might expect, given the political climate. The company wanted to deal with us directly. As it turned out, the company officials could communicate very well with us in English via email. It was in the spoken language where they had some minor difficulty. This, I found to be quite common in China as all schools teach a mandatory class in English, but the students don't get a great deal of verbal practice. So, we dropped the Taiwan rep, who became very angry about the loss since it was developing very rapidly into a profitable arrangement for both of us.

With our new partner reselling our products in China, we had found a ripe new market that developed very rapidly. However, in the third year of that partnership, I received an email from one of the principals in that original representative's company informing us that the other principal was working with a friend of his to copy our products! That, of course, is the greatest fear one has when selling in the free-for-all that is China.

Entrepreneurship is rampant. I likened it to the Wild West. But we were not about to abandon this market to a copy. We immediately cancelled our contract with the company, but I didn't think that would really stop the theft. However, this led directly to the next phase of our operations in China – our own direct sales office.

Having worked for a couple of years with the partner who disclosed the theft – and because of his honesty – I explored the possibility of him becoming our employee as manager of our own sales office. But I needed a business plan, something that was totally foreign to him. To put together the plan for presentation to our management team, I had to get the basics of what it cost to do business in China directly. From him, I got the cost of employees for office staff, the cost of a couple of engineers for service and application, office costs in the city of Nanjing, travel costs and other vital general and administrative expenses. I also needed the current selling price our products were being sold for in the Chinese market.

That last item was the shocker. Our selling price in China was 30 to 40% higher than our selling price in the U.S. market. After discounting the freight and duty costs, which he provided, I realized from the base market we already had in China that we could put a product cost on our China sales office that covered our U.S. manufacturing costs and most of our U.S. prorated G&A expenses and still have enough margin left over to cover the projected G&A expenses of the China office, including sales commissions, as well as a very nice profit! This was a "no brainer," as we say.

Management easily approved my next step, which was "where do we go from here?" What exactly did we need to do to make this a reality?

With management's go ahead to set up this operation, I contacted the U.S. Department of Commerce to get any assistance it could offer. It had an office in Shanghai, with which I made an appointment for discussions on my next trip to China. In addition, I contacted our corporate attorneys to see if they had any dealings with Chinese law partners. They also had a contact with a Canadian law company that had a Shanghai office staffed with both Canadian and Chinese lawyers.

With my export manager for assistance, I headed to China. We were joined in Shanghai by our new Chinese partner, whom I was determined to make an integral part of any planning we did. The meeting with the U.S. Commerce people was not too helpful. They basically told me to do all the things I already had done: find a good Chinese partner to work with and get together a workable business plan. We not only had all of this, but we also already had customers – the most important element of any business plan!

Our meeting with the attorney was much more fruitful. Here, we discussed the nuts and bolts of what we needed to do to set-up an office in Nanjing. The first thing we needed was an address, which we did not yet have. Then, we needed to contact the local district office in Jiangsu Province, of which Nanjing is the capital. There, we would get all the details of registering the company. We also found out that we could hire all of our employees through the local district office, which would cover their payroll expenses, including all of their benefits. This would relieve us of having to finance an accounting department and administer all the benefits required by law.

The law office provided us with a draft agreement from which we could choose several variations. We agreed on the contents, and a draft was prepared for our presentation to the Jiangsu bureau. A young Chinese attorney was assigned to us to travel the next morning by train to Nanjing to begin the process.

The morning after our arrival in Nanjing, we began the search for office space. Our new Chinese partner had already started the process before our arrival and had several prospects for us. In addition, the attorney had contacted some locations in buildings that allowed foreign companies to occupy.

The beginning of our search was not very encouraging. Most of the possibilities were pretty run down. I was quite concerned about our image for our customers, and I wanted to hire the best people we could find, which I calculated required a modern up-to-date office space. Finally, late that day, we came to a brand new tower building that was just opening in the heart of Nanjing. It was also the tallest building in the city. Since it was just opening, prices, as they always are in China, were very much negotiable, which our attorney handled well. We got a great deal.

The next morning, we signed a contract and were underway. We visited the local bureau and set up our legalities and payroll account. When I returned to the States, I made a presentation to our board of directors, which was well received.

The sales office that we opened in Nanjing was an instant success. By the time of our third year, about 30% of our corporate profit was made in China. This was way beyond any of our original expectations. But now, our major competitors from both the United States and Europe were setting up manufacturing facilities to lower their costs and expedite deliveries. Such an operation, which in China at that time could be 100% owned by the foreign company, is called a Wholly Foreign Owned Enterprise – WFOE.

To get this done, we had to make a number of changes. First of all, we had to find a building in which we could manufacture, after which we could apply to the local government for the necessary permits. We also decided that we would install a version of our company's business operating system in our China plant to better coordinate records. We hired a local accounting firm to handle all the required tax filings and our own accountant to coordinate these activities.

However, to make this really work, we knew we had to have a company-trained technician knowledgeable about our manufacturing and products to handle this work. Fortunately, I had on staff an engineer with years of experience who was willing to relocate to China for a number of years to get this underway. Coming up with a pay package for such an expatriate because of the tax consequences is no simple exercise. We had to hire an outside tax expert to calculate the adjusted net income to keep the employee whole since he would owe taxes in both the United States and China.

Since parts of the final product would be manufactured in both the United States and China, we also created an engineering part number system to identify the country of origin. Key components that would be critical to the product's performance would continue to be made in the United States to prevent the Chinese from gaining the technology to make those parts. All final assembly and quality control would be handled in China.

This all takes much more time than you would expect, but we finally got everything underway. We took one of our better engineers from our China sales office and put him in charge of all the manufacturing operations under the expatriate after bringing him to the United States for training in our own factory.

There are several key points that we learned from this experience. While China is a rapidly developing country (more cars were sold in China in 2008 than in the United States), it is still a place where the laws protecting your business can be pretty lax and where U.S. expatriates can feel pretty lonely.

Business-to-business selling makes operations in China somewhat easier. If you sell a technical product, your customers will most likely be trained engineers eager for the latest technology. Selling in China, even more so than in the United

States, is based very much on relationships. Once these relationships are developed, sales are quick to materialize. The key is having that local partner who knows how to maintain those relationships without bribery. "Gift giving" is a way of life in their business world. In the United States, it can be considered bribery and is illegal. So, you must be very explicit in the instruction to your salespeople over what is and is not permitted by your company.

As with our Taiwan agent, you can't rely on an existing partner from another market – even one as close as China and Taiwan – for the required skills.

Identify a local with an entrepreneurial personality and basic business skills and try to build a long-term relationship. Make that person an integral part of your planning. Also, identify a local attorney and a local accountant with whom you can work.

Rely on your own insights and learn from your partner in the market. This also means that you need to protect your product from copying theft. The attempt to copy our product failed because the copier didn't know the critical elements that spelled the difference between success and failure. His copies didn't work.

Be willing to experiment with new ideas that may be different than your own experience indicates. However, don't tolerate sloppy work and shortcuts that you know will not work in the long run. Build on solid fundamentals in setting up the business. Watch out for pirated software, which is rampant.

Have a solid business plan that provides a realistic model for sales and expenses.

Strive to build loyalty and trust for a long-term partnership.

Protect your designs from theft. Keep close control over the key elements of your designs.

I know that over the last few years the climate in China has changed and that other approaches may be required. When our company was bought out by investors, the China operation did not continue in the same way.

Bibliography

Champy, James. Ree*ngineering Management: The Mandate for New Leadership*. New York: HarperCollins, 1995.

Drucker, Peter F. *The Effective Executive*. New York: Harper & Row, 1967.

---. *Innovation and Entrepreneurship: Practice and Principals*. New York: Harper & Row, 1985.

Francis, Theo. "Why You Work for a Giant Company." *The Wall Street Journal,* April 7, 2017.

Garwood, Dave, and Michael Bane. *Shifting Paradigms: Reshaping the Future of Industry*. Marietta, GA: Dogwood, 1992.

Kessler, Andy. "How Video Games are Changing the Economy." *The Wall Street Journal,* Jan. 3, 2011.

Kierlin, Robert A. *The Power of Fastenal People: Why do Some Companies Thrive…While Other Companies Just Survive*. Poway, CA: First Pacific Enterprise, 1997.

Levitz, Jennifer, and Philip Shishkin. "More Workers Cite Age Bias After Layoff." *The Wall Street Journal*, March 11, 2009.

Milken, Michael, and Igor Tulchinsky. "How Technology Liberates Human Capital." *The Wall Street Journal,* April 12, 2017.

Tapscott, Don, and Anthony D. Williams. *Wikinomics: How Mass Collaboration Changes Everything*. New York: Penguin Group, 2006.

Tarrant, John J. *Drucker: The Man Who Invented the Corporate Society*. Boston: Cahners Books, 1976.

"Three Mile Island Accident Anniversary: Days of Crisis." *Harrisburg Patriot News,* March 27, 2015.

About the Author

John "Jack" Marino has more than thirty years of experience working in management at small, independently owned companies and five years of experience working in a mega corporation. He holds several U.S. patents and designed a product that is still selling some 45 years after its introduction. He earned his bachelor's degree in aeronautical engineering from Rensselaer Polytechnic Institute in 1960 and his master's degree in engineering from Penn State University in 1972. Perhaps his greatest accomplishment is his family. Jack has been married for 57 years to the love of his life, Jean. The two reside in the rolling hills of Pennsylvania, where he spends his time gardening and woodworking. He is the father of six successful children and "Grandpa Jack" to 16 loving grandchildren. This is his first book.

www.ingramcontent.com/pod-product-compliance
Lightning Source LLC
Chambersburg PA
CBHW071431180526
45170CB00001B/295